Tom!

Best Wishes

THE INVENTOR'S PUZZLE

Deciphering the Business of Product Innovation

MARK LAKE, PhD

Executive Consultant
EagleRock Consulting, Inc.
Erie, Colorado

THE INVENTOR'S PUZZLE
Deciphering the Business of Product Innovation

BY MARK LAKE, PHD

Published by EagleRock Consulting, Inc.
Erie, Colorado 80516
www.inventorspuzzle.com

Lake, Mark S.
  The Inventor's Puzzle: Deciphering the Business of Product Innovation by Mark Lake
  © 2009. 214 pp.
  ISBN 978-0-578-03347-1
  1. Business.   2. Invention.   3. Product innovation.   4. Title

Several copyrighted corporate logos and excerpts from other books are reproduced herein with footnote acknowledgements to the copyright holders and for the sole purpose of illustrating key points discussed in the book. Also, the author gratefully acknowledges the following copyright holders for permission to use their cartoon graphics under separate license agreements:

Doug Savage, for the *Savage Chicken* cartoon on p. 57.
Rube Goldberg, Inc., for the *Device for Walking on Icy Pavements* cartoon on p. 68.
CSL® CartoonStock, for the *Decorating on a Shoestring* cartoon on p. 103.
My Cartoon Gallery, for the *Good, Bad, and Ugly* cartoon on p. 121.
Patrick Hardin, for the *Caveman* cartoon on p. 140.
CSL® CartoonStock, for the *All Star Team* cartoon on p. 160.
CSL® CartoonStock, for the *Naked Company President* cartoon on p. 164.

Note: Web addresses cited herein for quick reference and to compliment published information sources could have changed since the time of publication.

This book is dedicated to my personal and professional families.

*Those to whom I am thankfully related
and those who thankfully relate to my work!*

Acknowledgments

My career and life are the accumulation of the wisdom and guidance that I have absorbed by a long list of mentors and associates along the way. Isaac Newton once said: "If I can see farther, it is because I stand on the shoulders of giants." With a sincere sense of humility, I know that my insights and perspectives into the world of product innovation business are as much the property of those who have taught and guided me, as they are the product of my own introspections and inspirations. To complete a list of people on whose shoulders I have stood would be tedious – maybe impossible – for me, and more importantly boring for you. However, I must acknowledge three key individuals on whose shoulders I have stood and whose wisdom and guidance has become the foundation of my own learning and teaching process.

First, I must acknowledge my father, K. O. (short for Kern Owen), who taught me a very basic lesson from which this book is derived. This would be my paraphrase of the lesson, as my dad wasn't a man to reduce his lessons to short phrases! *In life, you pay for your education and your ignorance – usually education is cheaper.* My dad gave college a try at the request of the War Department in 1943, and on his way to earning his wings as a command pilot in B-24 Liberator bombers at the tender age of 19. However, the formal version of education didn't suit him, so he focused his energy on absorbing knowledge and a keenly developed common sense and sense of humor through life's lessons. I am forever indebted to his example, and could not possibly have gained the insights that I convey herein without learning first from him how to absorb a helpful education out of the un-structured learning environment of life.

Second, I must acknowledge my long-time mentor, colleague, and friend, Martin Mikulas, who actually taught me how to engineer, a basic lesson that I somehow failed to learn at all three engineering schools from which I have degrees, and how to understand people's strengths and weaknesses and to help them, in a kind and gentle manor, to see both. Martin is a Professor Emeritus of the University of Colorado and a member of the National Academy of Engineering. In one of many moments during which he helped me to see myself more clearly, he told me: "Lake, you're more than an optimist. . . you're an *illogical positive-ist*." Maybe the best, backhanded compliment I've ever received. Over time, I've become a little less illogical in my optimistic views, but have never lost my Midwestern-born taproot of optimism, which is a key asset in the business of product innovation.

Third, I wish to acknowledge my wife and life's partner Bray who, as the Executive Director of a homeless-outreach organization, inspires me daily by helping many less-fortunate people find their personal pathway forward. From her example I have derived a profound sense that whatever you can see you can achieve, and it is this sense of personal empowerment that drives me forward in my own consulting business and that, God willing, will help our boys, Parrish and Keynes, to become positive and productive members of society when they grow up.

I would now like to extend a grateful hand of thanks to another group of people who have, more directly, helped me evolve this book from initial concept to a final product that is hopefully a readable, informative, and enjoyable discourse on the subject.

First, I wish to thank my mother, Barbara, who is my original inspiration for writing and is destined for sainthood for raising four siblings who actually love, respect, and maybe even revere each other. The miracle of her accomplishment is not just the healthy family relationships that she created, but also the fact that she did it, and continues to do so with an amazing amount of patience, grace, and good humor! From an early age, she also taught me to respect proper grammar, spelling, and penmanship. Although to her chagrin I never fully mastered any of these skills, I did learn to appreciate those who have and owe a great debt to her for bringing her mastery of them to bear on drafts of this book. She not only caught typos and miss-statements, but she gave me one of the best pieces of editorial advice I received on this project – to give the book a simple and memorable title! Thanks mom, "Brunelleschi's Dome" just wouldn't have caught on!

I also wish to thank my sister Sharon who shares with me a professional connection into the world of product innovation business, and with whom I debated, discussed, and ultimately honed my original vision for this book. Her keen insights into this business sector, coupled with her creative talents for writing, left an indelible impression on me and helped me refine my own concept for how this book should be written. Almost like a golf coach, Sharon helped me shape my *writing swing* - the style in which this book is written – to get rid of the slice and the hook and send the message right down the middle of the fairway. If I've done that, and made the book easier and more entertaining to read, then we both owe Sharon for her sharp editorial eye and tutoring skills!

Furthermore, I wish to extend a warm and hearty thanks to a group of friends, colleagues, and professional acquaintances who happily agreed to review a draft of this book and provide me with an early glimpse into the reactions that I could expect out of its future readers. In no particular order, I wish to thank James Arkebauer, Brian Hayes, Richard Lazar, Jeffrey Petrozzino, Linda Bresnahan, Rory Barrett, Ken Gall, Kurt Jacobus, Carlos Smith, and Tammy Lake. Their collective thoughts and insights allowed me to tweak and adjust the draft to cover more completely the important subject matter of the book and more perfectly address these issues to the intended audience. Every one of these reviewers is an expert in some dimension of innovation and/or small business development. As such, I also owe them all a debt of gratitude for providing a collective litmus test over the accuracy of the book's content and its conclusions.

Additionally, I have to single out the one person who helped me most in creating an image that best conveys the theme for this book, Jason Metter.[1] Jason is a graphic artist, web designer, and book designer extraordinaire who patiently sat with me while I explained the litany of intangible pieces of this puzzle that I was struggling to express in words. Miraculously, Jason brought those intangible pieces together in a very effective piece of cover art that better captures the essence of this book than I could have possibly captured in words alone. His contribution to this work is indelible, and I gratefully thank him for showing me how the right picture is worth *more than* a thousand words!

Finally, I absolutely must acknowledge every writer's best friend the coffee shop. Indeed, if it weren't for such a place where I can escape the dull roar of life around my house, savor the smells and enjoy the taste of my favorite rich dark beverage while surfing the Web, this book might

---

[1] www.bluefruit.com

Acknowledgments

never have seen the light of day. Although I owe a thanks to several such establishments, I must single out a favorite one, Vic's Espresso and Coffee House in Longmont Colorado whose proprietor Whitey DeBroux, a self-proclaimed frustrated inventor, provided many delicious drinks with a side order of inspirational conversation and a welcoming environment in which to write!

Contents

THE INVENTOR'S PUZZLE

Deciphering the Business of Product Innovation

Preface

"When I was a boy of 14, my father was so ignorant I could hardly stand to have the old man around. But when I got to be 21, I was astonished at how much the old man had learned in seven years!"

– Mark Twain

Have you ever been struck by an idea for how to make a "better mousetrap"? Maybe you've dreamed of a portable caddy that could carry your coffee cup and free your hands to answer your cell phone on the subway, or maybe an application for your iPod that automatically alerts you when your favorite band is performing near your home. If you are prone to these moments of inventive genius then you have also doubtlessly spent hours dreaming of getting rich quick off of just one of those clever ideas! Indeed, this daydream is probably the purest form of the American Dream, and it is the dream that drives the world of product innovation business.

Every year in this country billions of dollars are invested in creating new inventions and launching new businesses that will turn those inventions into market-ready products. Many of these new product innovation businesses are launched and led by the inventor who had the original vision for the new product, but who generally lacks a solid basis of experience in the product innovation business world. As such, many of these start-up enterprises fail - not due to a bad idea, but due to bad business planning and execution.

The purpose of this book is to convey a collection of observations, perspectives, wisdom, perceptions, accumulated experiences, warnings, etc., that collectively decipher the world of successful product innovation business. In particular, this book exposes five essential issues that arise when evolving an invention from the point of conception through the development and marketing of practical products based on the invention. The nature of these five issues is

1

exposed one by one like the pieces of a puzzle. Then, the pieces are interconnected in an effort to explain how to build a successful product innovation business.

This book was written for the myriad of prospective stakeholders in product innovation businesses including the would-be inventors, entrepreneurs, and investors who are drawn to this type of business, but who might lack first-hand experience with such a business. If your interest is to become personally involved in this business sector, then this book should serve as a top-level instruction manual or a self-help guide of sorts. If your interest is to learn about this business sector for academic reasons, then this book should serve as a first primer on the subject and the references that are included throughout will help to identify key topics that are worthy of further study.

Regardless of your specific interests, I assume that you are drawn to this subject because you have a certain amount of interest in the genius that creates new inventions and the business acumen that turns such inventions into profitable enterprises. If this assumption is correct, then I am happy to make your acquaintance, and I am hopeful that you will find insights in this book that will be of value as you move forward in your pursuits.

Now that I assert to know something about you, let me tell you a few things about myself in order for you to understand my perspectives on, and experiences with, this business sector. My business is to consult with inventors and the leaders of small, product innovation companies who are having a wide variety of, but consistently very similar, difficulties in getting good ideas and inventions brought into the marketplace. This book is a natural extension of that consulting enterprise. Indeed by writing this book I hope that I can reach out to a broader community of young inventors and product innovation business leaders and help that community to become more successful in their early endeavors.

Why do I work in this business sector? Because I love the process of learning, discovery, and scientific investigation that is central to all product innovation enterprises; and I have a natural appreciation for the myriad of challenges that plague such enterprises. As much as I love the process of learning, I also love the process of teaching, which is what drew me to become a consultant in the first place. To a degree, this book is an expression of my love of teaching. It also reflects my style of teaching – a mixture of insight and irreverence, sprinkled with a healthy amount of historical references and humor. Hopefully the book is fine-tuned to keep your attention long enough that you learn without actually feeling the pain of learning!

One of my clients refers to me as "the old guy." Since I am ONLY 48 years old, my vanity was originally offended by this comment. However upon reflection, I decided this was a high compliment. After all, the average age of this company's staff – a very vibrant, energetic, forward-moving, high-tech organization – is approximately 30 years old. So, of course I am the old guy! More importantly, I have been there and done that, and to them, that experience is high capital. Thanks for the endorsement guys. I'll wear the title of "old guy" with pride!

How did I ever become the old guy? Well in short, I've spent a lot of years in school – certainly more than I ever planned to at the outset. I also spent a lot of years working for the Federal Government – NASA more specifically, and a lot of years in private industry. Along the way, I have had the good fortune to be associated with several universities in ad hoc and adjunct faculty capacities, through which I have had access to a steady stream of new ideas and energetic people who are developing those ideas. Finally, my professional journey has been such that I have had a grand total of 10 different mailing addresses over the 25-year expanse of my career, including zip codes in all four time zones within the Continental U.S. (boy I'd love to find work in Hawaii!). In total, I've done a lot over a long period of time, and in a lot of places, so it's fair – heck, it's a compliment - to be called the old guy.

My approach to consulting is very hands-on. Rather than being content to offer high-level guidance and general philosophical advice, I seek out clients who welcome a more intimate involvement by me in their enterprise. I prefer to roll up my sleeves and get directly into the daily grind, as this level of involvement is often necessary in order to see where the problems really lie. Ultimately I am a doer and, as I believe my clients would attest, I am not content to simply identify a problem, but very driven to work out and implement solutions that best fit the situation at hand. Indeed this accumulated experience from trouble shooting real-world problems in product innovation businesses provides the foundation of information on which this book is built.

I hope that my hands-on approach to business consulting is reflected in the style that I have written this book. Rather than discussing the concepts as an academic might, from a distance and relying mainly on impartial analysis of statistical data, I have intentionally written this book in a more conversational style and from a much closer, first-hand perspective. I chose this style of writing because it is comfortable for me, and hopefully more entertaining and informative for you. Most importantly, I chose this personal style of writing because it conveys the subliminal message that *people* determine success in product innovation business not just academic *theories*.

So, now you know a bit more about me and why I have written this book. I assert that I know something about you and your motivations, and will work hard to convey the ideas in this book to you as personally as my distant appreciation for you will allow. I won't profess here to give you every bit of knowledge or every detail of information that will be essential to your success in product innovation business. Rather, I will occasionally point you at other references where you will find a deeper treatment of key issues, and I will confine this book to a higher-level, and somewhat philosophical, treatment of the problem of how to take an invention or new idea into the marketplace.

To accomplish this, I have organized the book as follows. In Chapter 1, I will clean the slate (so to speak) by discussing, and in some cases dispelling, preconceptions about what it takes to be successful in product innovation businesses. I will de-construct a key element – the inventor's passion for the invention – and show how it can either drive the enterprise forward or impede the path forward. Furthermore, I will discuss in broad terms other factors that contribute to success and failure in the enterprise, and will conclude by explaining business management concepts that are critical to all successful product innovation businesses.

In Chapter 2, I will provide a description of the entire process from invention to commercialization and the five basic issues, or pieces to *The Inventor's Puzzle*. To do this in a way that will hopefully settle in your mind as almost instinctive insights and a new level of common sense, I will tell a very real story of invention and commercial success. However, to avoid making this story dry, stale, and un-interesting, I will tell a story that occurred 600 years ago – the design and construction by Filippo

Preface

Brunelleschi (pronounced like *Broonl-eskee*) of the great dome over the cathedral of Santa Marie del Fiore in Florence Italy. I hope you will find both entertainment in this historical business metaphor and key insights into the pieces of *The Inventor's Puzzle*, which you must master if you are to succeed in your own business enterprise.

Chapters 3 through 7 will address the five pieces of *The Inventor's Puzzle*, respectively, and will build on the insights that I hope to give you in Chapter 2. I have organized these chapters in a *pseudo-chronological* order – the rough order in time when these issues will dominate your thought process and actions as you move forward toward realizing your goals. Seen from a slightly different perspective, Chapters 3-7 present each of five *cardinal sins* – not sins born out of evil, but rather sins born out of ignorance - that I find very often perpetrated by young, aspiring inventors, who are hoping to create a product out of their idea. So, in total, these chapters serve to alert you to the pitfalls of these cardinal sins, while also helping you to understand what to do to avoid these mistakes and put your efforts on a path towards success.

Finally, Chapter 8 will describe two final elements that are key to your success – the creation of an exit strategy or end goal for the enterprise, and the establishment of practices that will allow you to deal with the inevitable and unpredictable challenges along the way. If left alone, these nagging problems can easily bring your enterprise to a halt as surely as ignoring any of the five basic pieces of the puzzle will bring about failure. Furthermore, without a clearly defined end goal in mind, the likelihood of success is remote.

At the start of every chapter I have included a favorite quote that captures, to a degree, the theme or central message of the chapter. I have included these quotes because I think they can serve to help you remember, and make sense of, the central message of the chapter. The famous line from Mark Twain that I have included at the beginning of this Preface is a personal favorite, and one that I recite often and in many situations. I am drawn to it, and have included it here because I think that we are all initially motivated to move into product innovation business by a combination of ignorance and arrogance – ignorance of what lies ahead, and arrogance to plow forward regardless. Rather than being ashamed of this I think we should embrace it as the essential ingredient that causes an inventor to invent and then to see a business opportunity grow out of the invention.

In total, I hope that this book will help replace some ignorance with knowledge and common sense about the world of product innovation business – a perspective from which you can more instinctively anticipate issues and problems as they are about to occur, and more efficiently act to put these issues to rest. If this book serves that purpose, and after having read it, you find that you are more confident and capable to become successful in your endeavors, then it will have been a success. If through this book you come to some new-found perspectives or vantage points that help you see forward and maneuver around obstacles better and that ultimately enable you to have the insight to realize your vision, then you will have helped me to move into a new dimension of my own consulting career – to coach a broader audience of young inventors and entrepreneurs!

If you believe in karma, and I believe that you should if you are to be successful in any business, then you will also appreciate that part of my motivation in writing this book derives from a sense of community obligation to help other small-business leaders succeed. The truth of it is that I teach my clients but I also learn from my clients as well. As I accumulate more knowledge and experience through each new business case study, I naturally translate this expanding experience base into greater insights and a wider range of tactics for future clients. This symbiosis is part of the win-win proposition that drives me to excel as a consultant and allows my clients to succeed when I succeed.

Ultimately, in writing this book your success is my first motivation. If you are unsuccessful, then my efforts are for naught. The only equity stake that I seek here is a part of the back-end satisfaction of having contributed to your success – an opportunity to share in the feeling of accomplishment that will undoubtedly serve to justify all of your hard work and painfully learned lessons along the way. If you find that this book does help in your journey forward, then look me up, offer to buy me a coffee, and I will enjoy the opportunity to hear your personal story. If on the other hand this book leads you astray, look me up and I'll guarantee to reimburse you the money that you paid for the book. There's a deal that you will NEVER get from another business consultant – a money-back guarantee!

– Mark Lake
October 2009
Erie, Colorado

1

Preconceptions About Inventors and Product Innovation Businesses

"Genius is 1 percent inspiration and 99 percent perspiration."

–Thomas Edison

The national economy is in a state of collapse. Following a period of unmatched economic growth during which this country saw unprecedented expansion of the business base accompanied by an abnormal growth of speculation in the finance and banking sectors, the country was plunged headfirst into a catastrophic state of economic recession. The trigger moment for the sudden collapse was the failure of a national banking firm of impeccable reputation. The immediate consequences of the collapse included dramatic contraction in key business sectors, devaluing of goods and services, and a general state of timidity on the part of the investment capital groups in the country.

Against this backdrop of economic crisis an unknown inventor found good cause to start a business around a singularly clever idea. Much like the wild flower seed that defies logic to find root in the rarified air of the high alpine tundra, this idea took hold and a business started to grow and flourish around it precisely at a time when all economic forces seemed to be allied against such an enterprise. Imagine seeing twenty years into the future and the economic crisis has passed giving way to another era of economic expansion and growth. In this expanse of time, the invention has triggered the development of an entirely new market and the company has grown to become one of the most successful publicly traded companies in the country.

Is it possible that just such an idea is being conceived of or such a business is being launched at this moment? If history is any guide to the future then the answer is yes.

You see, the scenario just described actually happened in this country over 130 years ago. The economic crisis was the so-called Financial Panic of 1873[2], the unknown inventor was Thomas Alva Edison, his invention was the incandescent light bulb, and the company that he founded to commercialize that invention would come to be known as the General Electric Corporation, which by 1896 had succeeded in becoming one of the first twelve publically owned companies registered on the newly formed Dow Jones Industrial Average. Indeed, Edison's story of invention and business development is now well accepted as one of the most remarkable examples of how ingenuity, coupled with good business practice, can overcome even the dourest of economic climates.[3]

A bad economy can mean good business

The purpose of this chapter is to prepare a clean slate upon which to begin building insight into the world of *product innovation business* – where the business is about developing and marketing new inventions. As someone who has chosen to read this book, you are someone who might already have a degree of insight into business and/or the processes of invention and product innovation. However, unless you have already built such a business yourself and succeeded in the enterprise, you might also carry with you some baggage in the way of preconceptions that bias your views and could stand in the way of gaining a better understanding of this realm of business.

So, to start with I want to challenge a commonly held belief that it is a bad idea to start a new business during a down economy. Although this belief is valid for some business sectors (e.g., I wouldn't think of starting a construction company in today's flat real estate market), this adage is simply not applicable to the world of product innovation business. Edison proved it 130 years ago, and countless other innovators

---

[2] From: *The Great Republic by the Master Historians, Vol. III,* by Hubert H. Bancroft (ed.), [http://www.publicbookshelf.com/public_html/The_Great_Republic_By_the_Master_Historians_Vol_III/panicof1_hd.html]

[3] Stacy Perman, "Recession Lessons," *Business Week,* [http://images.businessweek.com/ss/09/04/0410_recession_lessons/index.htm]

including electronic giants Bill Hewlett and David Packard, software king Bill Gates, and cable-TV magnate Ted Turner, have repeated the pattern of launching hugely successful product innovation companies in depressed economies.

> A depressed economy provides a fertile environment for invention and product innovation. Economic depression forces people to re-evaluate old norms and consider new alternatives. Old markets built on old products and technologies tend to erode in rough economic times and give way to new markets built on new product paradigms.

In this way, the Financial Panic of 1873 gave way to an economic revolution[4] that created many new markets for goods and services, including a new industry that made Thomas Edison rich and one that we all take for granted today – the electric utility industry.

Inspiration versus perspiration

Thanks to Thomas Edison's archetypical invention, the cartoon metaphor for the moment of invention is a light bulb usually depicted glowing brightly in a thought bubble above the would-be inventor's head. Sometimes the moment of invention is just that – a moment. Sometimes, it consumes a larger expanse of time – more like a dimly lit bulb that is gradually brought to life by a steadily increasing electrical current. Regardless of the elapsed time of the event, I prefer to think of the moment of invention as the moment of *conception* because *invention* sounds so final as if all the hard work has been done! Whereas *conception* really alerts us to the fact that, to be blunt, the work has just begun!

If you have kids, like I do, then you can't help but immediately think about them when you say the word conception. You automatically associate conception with the instant at which your life changed. Kids are a life-altering experience, plain and simple. Few of us who have kids

---

[4] *The Age of the Economic Revolution, 1876-1900*, by Carl N. Degler, Glenview, IL (1967)

actually knew how much energy and time they would take before we had them. Maybe this bit of deception is part of nature's plan – right?! The point is that parenthood can be described as moments of unparalleled joy interspersed among hours of unparalleled frustration! In a similar way, nurturing a new invention from concept to market-ready product involves an almost unfair balance between joy and frustration.

Thomas Edison's classic quote, which is recited at the beginning of this chapter, represents a *rough-order-of-magnitude* – accurate to about a factor of ten – estimate of where efforts must be focused in order to bring a new invention to the market by building a business around that invention. Sadly, only a relatively small fraction (maybe between 1/1000 and 1/10) of one's time and creative energies are going to be devoted to that thing that probably brings the inventor the most joy – the inspiration that leads to creating a new invention. The overwhelming majority of time and energy will be invested in addressing a vast array of business challenges that would otherwise prevent the invention from ever seeing the light of day as a viable product.

A wealthy acquaintance of mine who invests money in product innovation businesses told me once that, on average, only 1% of the total price of most products that are currently in the market is devoted to the research and development of that product. The remaining 99% is consumed by manufacturing, distribution, marketing and sales, etc.! As an inventor and engineer myself, that number is humbling. It kind of makes me think that I should have studied a different field in college, like maybe marketing and sales for example!

Whether you chose to take it from Thomas Edison or my friend the business financier, the fact remains that the part of the problem that we inventors tend to enjoy the most – the inspiration that gives way to a new invention – represents a small fraction of the total process that is necessary to create a good, and money-making business enterprise out of a good idea. We love our inventions and ideas as sincerely and completely as a parent loves his or her child. However, in order for an invention to see the light of day as a marketable product, it HAS to be matured through a protracted period of "adolescence" and "early adulthood."

If you are an inventor and you interpret Thomas Edison's quote as a warning sign: "Beware – all of the fun is over once you've come up with the idea," then my best advice for you is to very consciously and intently ignore your creative ideas before they ever get out of your own mind and into someone else's mind. There is no dishonor in walking away from your own thoughts. For all I know, there might even be a section of psychology entirely devoted to this type of behavior in inventors (something that portrays denial as a healthy defense mechanism, I suspect).

Regardless of psychological norms, if you read Thomas Edison's quote and feel depressed, then I say stop reading this book right now. Put it quietly on the shelf and walk away. Better yet, put a $1 sticker on this book and sell it at the next garage sale. You will sleep better at night. You will have a happier marriage – with or without kids. Most importantly, you will never have to suffer through the life-altering experience that all successful inventors suffer through – solving the challenging puzzle of how to turn their ideas into practical, and marketable, products.

If you are not an inventor, but are interested in the world of product innovation business, then I walk you through this brief exposé on the psychology of inventors to help you appreciate an often-misunderstood element of successful product innovation businesses. The very force that inspires an inventor to create something new and to launch a business around that idea – passion for the invention – is also the force that can destroy the business.

Passion is a volatile commodity that breeds parochialism and elitism, and if left unbalanced by good business sense, passion alone will undermine the efforts of inventors and entrepreneurs who wish to capitalize on their inventions. Most inventors develop an attachment to their creations as strong as the paternal attachment that a father has for his son. However, almost all inventions must evolve substantially if they are to become commercially viable products, and few inventors have the instincts to entrust their inventions to others who have the experience to thus evolve the invention into a product.

If I could paraphrase Edison's famous quote in a way that might steer the inventor and would-be businessperson in a direction to properly focus her passions and energies, I might paraphrase the quote as follows:

A successful inventor derives about 1 percent of her joy and passion from the inspiration that created the invention, and about 99 percent of her joy and passion out of the perspiration associated with bringing that invention to the market.

It's not as concise and memorable as Mr. Edison's version, but I think it's a bit more practical and helpful to an inventor and would-be businessperson who is standing at the moment of conception of a new idea, and trying to mentally prepare herself for the challenges of converting that idea into a profitable business. I believe firmly that most inventors who build successful companies around their inventions not only find joy in the moment of conception of the idea, but they find joy in the hours, weeks, and maybe years of time they spend in mastering the process of bringing that idea to fruition in practical products.

It is well known that Edison himself derived enormous pleasure and satisfaction out of the drudgery of turning a good idea into a practical product.[5] In fact, after several years of painstaking work and prior to discovering a truly practical version of the light bulb that could be turned on and off thousands of times without burning out the filament, he happily reported with a grin:

> *"We have not failed. . . We now know a thousand ways <u>not</u> to build a light bulb!"* – Thomas Edison

A financial consequence of the 99% perspiration rule is that the inventor will most likely have to give up a substantial fraction of his ownership interest in the invention in order to entice others to join in the enterprise. The following pie charts depict how the inventor's ownership will dilute from the entire pie to a small piece of the pie as the invention is matured from concept to product. Other people who will gain a piece of the pie might include key advisors who help to structure and guide the enterprise (e.g., members of a Board of Directors), investors who provide cash to move the enterprise forward, and finally key employees

---

[5] *Edison on Innovation: 102 Lessons in Creativity for Business and Beyond,* by Alan Axelrod, John Wiley and Sons (2008)

of the business who will collectively provide a significant portion of the 99% worth of perspiration necessary to bring the invention to market.

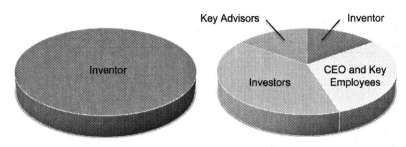

Inventor's equity at the moment of conception.

Dilution of inventor's equity on the way to commercialization.

At first glance, this dilution of ownership might seem unfair. After all, the inventor created the idea without the help of all of these people. Why should they benefit so substantially from his genius? Well, this is the price that must be paid for the 99% worth of perspiration that nurtures any invention from conception to commercialization. Few if any inventors have the ability to do it all themselves. Even Edison diluted his personal ownership in all of his inventions in order to build a massive corporate empire that ultimately made him wealthy beyond his original dreams.

Do you have to build a business to cash in on a new invention?

For the most part, this book is built from the single cornerstone assumption that you, the inventor or would-be entrepreneur, wish to make money by building up some type of business enterprise around a particular invention. Through the course of this book I will discuss the general problem of building a successful product innovation business enterprise and highlight several specific scenarios through which you might capitalize on a new invention. However, before we invest the time to explore all of these details, it is important to address the very basic question: do you have to build a business to cash in on a new invention?

In short, the answer is no. In fact, it is quite common for inventors to sell their ideas to others who might lack their flare for creativity but who have a flare for product innovation business. Indeed, numerous books discuss how to license inventions in order to reap financial rewards without suffering the cost and risk of building a business.[6] As you will discover through the course of this book, building a successful business to develop and market a new invention is no trivial task. As such, it makes a great deal of sense for any inventor to consider selling her invention to someone else and avoiding many of the challenges associated with building a business around that invention. However, before you decide that selling out early is the best option for you, realize that this option is not pain free.

When you sell a used car, you have to know something about the customers and the competition in order to set a fair price that you can be reasonably sure of getting. In the same sense, selling your invention to a company that might develop and market new products derived from the invention demands that you understand what such a company is willing to pay. Appreciating what such a company might pay requires that you understand the market for your invention, which will be discussed in Chapter 3, and the costs that the company might incur in developing the invention, which will be discussed in Chapters 5 through 7.

Furthermore, just as it is essential that you have a clear title, or proof of ownership, to your car before you attempt to sell it, you must be able to demonstrate that you own the invention – or rather the *intellectual property* that constitutes the invention – before you will be able to entice a company to buy the invention from you. In Chapter 4, I will talk about how you can establish clear ownership over your invention and how your invention can be sold or licensed to a company who will develop and market products from the invention.

Ultimately, as I will discuss in Chapter 8, it is important for you to decide your "exit strategy", or how you want to cash in on the invention. Do you want to pursue an early licensing agreement that might bring less value but that presents much less risk and cost? Do you want to develop a viable product, establish its market appeal, and then sell the rights to further produce and market the product? Or do you want to build a business that will develop, produce, and market the product

---

[6]For example see: *How to License Your Million Dollar Idea: Everything You Need to Know To Turn a Simple Idea into a Million Dollar Payday*, by Harvey Reese, John Wiley & Sons (1993)

indefinitely, and create for you a long-term source of revenue and wealth?

> Regardless of which exit strategy best fits your needs, being successful in capitalizing on your invention demands that you become savvy about what it takes to build a product innovation business.

Hence, I will discuss all aspects of the problem as if you were planning to build the business yourself. From this vantage point, I hope that you will come to see the challenges and risks, as well as the potential rewards, with sufficient clarity that you can decide whether to seek an early sale of your invention or to take on the task of building a business around it.

Do you have what it takes to succeed in product innovation business?

Let me now debunk a myth that to be successful in business, you have to have an *MBA* – Masters Degree in Business Administration. If you have an MBA you likely have already amassed many of the skills and knowledge that are necessary to lead small, product innovation businesses through the process of development and marketing of new inventions. However, if you don't already have an MBA, don't think that you need to spend two years getting one before you can launch your own business enterprise or seek out a customer to buy the rights to your invention. After all, Bill Gates dropped out of Harvard as an undergraduate student to start Microsoft!

> The most important personal attributes for success in product innovation business are enthusiasm, an honest understanding of your own limitations or lack of knowledge (regardless of diplomas hanging on the wall), and a willingness to interact with and learn from others in the business.

Certainly, success in product innovation businesses requires mastery of several specific topics that will be addressed in this book, but the overarching requirement is a good business sense and a healthy amount of personal drive – the 99% perspiration part. You have probably heard the phrase "self-made millionaire" right? This title is usually applied to a person who, without the help of a formal education, was able to build a healthy personal fortune in the business world mainly guided by good business sense and a healthy amount of personal drive! Come to think of it, I guess Bill Gates would technically be called a self-made *billionaire*!

Motivation and business sense are necessary, but by themselves not sufficient to ensure your success. In general, I have also found that most successful product innovation businesspeople are *extroverts* – very outgoing and talkative, especially when it comes to talking about their ideas. The business world is an extremely social world. Healthy and constant interactions with other businesspeople, customers, and a myriad of prospective partners are a key to your success. If you are an inventor and are more comfortable in your garage tinkering on your inventions than talking with someone about your inventions in a coffee shop, then you need to find a partner early on who sees your vision and can help build the relationships that you will need to succeed.

Moreover, I am convinced that the most successful businesspeople are the ones who truly understand their own *limitations* – lack of knowledge/experience – and who are dedicated to either learn the things that they don't already know about or delegate these responsibilities to people who already know. Sometimes the hardest part of being successful in business is balancing your confidence and determination to move forward with a healthy self-evaluation and a thoughtful consideration of the question "do I know enough to move forward and be successful?"

Assuming that you have the right combination of personality traits and skills to be successful, or you are prepared to ally yourself with others who compliment your skills, what are the other factors that could cause your business to succeed or fail? Well, I suppose this is a "glass-half-full vs. glass-half-empty" kind of question. First let's take a quick look at the empty half of the glass – the causes of failure among small businesses. Then I will devote the rest of this book to the full half of the glass – concepts and practices that will lead to success in your business.

Why do product innovation businesses fail?

As I mentioned in the Preface to this book, every year in this country billions of dollars are invested in the development of new inventions and products with the hope of launching successful businesses around those new products. The vast majority of these new business enterprises are launched and led by the inventor who had the original vision for the new product or technology, but who generally lacks a solid basis of experience in the small-business world. As such, the vast majority of these enterprises fail - not due to a bad idea, but due to bad business planning and execution.

Annually, the U.S. Department of Labor, and most state governments (usually through the Secretary of State's office, or the Governor's Office of Economic Development) compile statistics regarding business startups and failures. If you have the interest you can certainly spend hours reading these publically available reports, but I'm not sure that you will find in them the root-cause issues that lead to business failures. As I review these resources, the best statistical summary I have been able to compile is that every year approximately three to four million new businesses of all types (including, but not limited to, product innovation businesses) are launched in this country. Roughly one-third of these businesses ultimately succeed in becoming profitable; one-third of them break even; and one-third of them fail in one way or another.

The National Federation of Independent Business (NFIB),[7] a leading small business association and government-lobbying group, has found that more than two-thirds of all small businesses start up in the owner's home, and only 21% initially employ someone besides the owner. Does this sound familiar? The *NFIB Small Business Policy Guide*,[8] reports that about half of startup businesses cease to exist within five years after they open. However, the reasons for closure or failure are vast and complex and sometimes even unintuitive when just looking at the bare statistics. For example, the study found that a sale or merger of a business might be interpreted as a "failure" in some statistical studies because the business closed its doors. So in short, it is difficult to derive conclusive trends from government statistics, but these statistics do serve to help you understand basic probabilities of success and failure.

---

[7] www.nfib.com
[8] http://www.nfib.com/object/2753115.html

Anecdotally, my own experiences with product innovation businesses leads me to conclude that there are five basic reasons why such businesses tend to fail outright or only achieve a modest degree of success (i.e., hit a break-even point). These reasons boil down to the following:

Product innovation businesses fail when the inventor and/or business leaders lack:

1. a clear understanding of the market for their idea;
2. clear and defendable ownership rights over their idea;
3. the ability to develop the idea into an "engineered" product;
4. the money required to finance the business enterprise; and/or
5. the necessary team to make it all happen.

I will discuss business failure scenarios further in Chapter 8, but for now just recognize that missing out on just one of these top five issues, will likely lead to failure – perhaps not immediately, but ultimately. At best, missing out on just one of these issues is a recipe for breaking even or just managing to stay afloat in the business world. Indeed, these five issues define the five pieces of *The Inventor's Puzzle*, and the remainder of this book will be an exercise in learning how to address these issues adequately in your business enterprise.

Why do product innovation businesses succeed?

Inventors tend to think that the more cleaver or better the invention, the more likely it will become a successful product. Good ideas seem to pop up everywhere, but how many of those good ideas are actually developed into marketable products? I don't know the exact statistics, but would guess less than one out of a hundred!

Conversely, how many successful businesses have built huge fortunes on marketing inferior products? Well, the number is staggering and continues to grow. It seems that the marketing of inferior products is becoming more the norm than the exception nowadays. For example, have you ever heard of the marketing concept of "planned obsolescence?"[9] Indeed, many of the products that you buy today are intentionally designed to be *obsolete* – to require replacement – in a relatively short period of time. It's a great way for a product development company to keep in the business of developing new products!

Clearly, there is not much correlation between the quality or novelty of the invention and the likelihood that it will become a marketable product for a successful business. The basic truth is this:

> Product innovation businesses succeed when, *regardless of the novelty of the invention,* there is a good opportunity for the product to capture a significant amount of the market, and the business is thoughtfully structured with proper leadership to grab that opportunity.

The balance of this book is devoted to deconstructing this statement into its essential elements. At this point, suffice it to say that any person who has invented something for which there is a good market opportunity, and thoughtfully applies the same level of passion and energy in addressing each of the five issues listed in the last subsection as she applied in creating the invention, can expect to succeed in the business world. Of course, the devil is in the details, and success isn't as simple as reading a short list of issues and then quickly developing a plan of action to address these issues.

The five pieces of *The Inventor's Puzzle* seem simple, but figuring out how to take action to address these issues can be difficult – especially to one who lacks some basic experience in the small-business world. In our everyday life we are constantly met with unusual situations that we have learned to deal with using our general knowledge and common sense. In the world of product innovation business I contend that general knowledge is insufficient and common sense is oftentimes counterintuitive. So applying general knowledge and commonsense

---

[9] *Made to Break: Technology and Obsolescence in America,* by Giles Slade, Harvard University Press (2006)

practices that we have learned in our every-day world to the world of product innovation business can lead to very bad consequences.

Several years ago, a group of private investors organized the Entrepreneurial Standards Forum to explore the root causes of failure and success in product innovation businesses and to develop a series of online tools for entrepreneurs and investors to assess the risk of any particular business enterprise.[10]   These online tools compare key characteristics of your business to the same characteristics from a database of successful businesses, define a "success path" that your business can take forward, and tell you where you are on this path. Finally, the tools provide a comprehensive assessment of risks and opportunities for a full range of entrepreneurial ventures, including startups, emerging growth companies, and new business units within established businesses.

Even at this early stage, I think you can gain some very powerful insights into what might make your business enterprise successful by visiting the Entrepreneurial Standards Forum website, filling out the survey, and reading the reports that are generated. Beyond that, just be patient as I will come back to the question of how to succeed and how to avoid failure throughout this book. Ultimately, in the last chapter I will bring all of these concepts together in a way that should help you see much more clearly what path you should take forward to maximize your chances of succeeding.

Misconceptions in the language of product innovation business

A final topic that I want to address in this chapter is that of key words that are frequently used in the vocabulary of product innovation businesses and the often-unintuitive meanings of these words. I want to go through this exercise for two reasons. First, I want to help you begin to build your business lexicon and appreciation for a few unintuitive concepts that are critical to success in product innovation business. Second, throughout the remainder of this book I will use these words to

---

[10] http://es2f.org/

explain many critical concepts, so I want to do what I can now to avoid misinterpretations or misunderstandings later.

Invention versus product. What is the difference between an invention and a product? You might casually interchange the words, but in this book I am going to be utterly clear in their use.

> An *invention* is an idea that nobody has thought of before. Whereas, a *product* is something that is either already in the marketplace or on its way to the marketplace and that serves a specific need among the buying public.

If drawing this clean line seems pedantic to you, then please reread lesson number one presented a few pages back: *many small, product innovation businesses fail simply because the inventor lacks a clear understanding of the market for that invention (i.e., a marketable product that can be created from the invention).*

In my view, there are two types of creative people: those who create for the pure joy and satisfaction of it, and those who create driven by these motives PLUS the added motivation of utility. In the first camp of creative people are the artists, musicians, sculptors, and actors among us. In the second camp of creative people are the architects, engineers, scientists, and – yes indeed – the inventors among us. But a successful inventor – in the likeness of Thomas Edison – is one who creates ideas that can be reduced to products that have value in the marketplace. In Chapter 3, I will describe the process of understanding the market for your invention, and hopefully will arm you with the insights that will allow you to better assess whether it is just a clever invention or one that also has true product potential.

Entrepreneur versus businessperson. I have often heard people casually claim that any good businessperson can manage any business – WRONG. There are many good businesspeople who understand the norms of particular types of businesses, and who have the organizational skills to oversee many types of businesses, but there are many fewer people who have those same skills and an aptitude and appetite for creating new business around an innovative new product.

In my view, a rare type of businessperson is *the entrepreneur*. Anyone who starts a business has some degree of the entrepreneurial spirit. But most successful product innovation businesses are, by definition, led by true *entrepreneurs*. Unlike the garden-variety good businessperson, *entrepreneurs* are bored with business-as-usual and scoff at the business norms that have already been reduced to textbook practice. They thrive on the unknowns of a new-business enterprise wrapped around an innovative product concept. They thirst to know where and how such a product might best fit in the market, and they measure success in their ability to solve very challenging problems that break down barriers to entry for these products into the market.

An *entrepreneur* is to the process of creating the successful product innovation business as the *inventor* is to the process of creating the new product idea.

Occasionally, though rarely, inventors make good entrepreneurs. There really are no formal requirements for the role of entrepreneur. There is only a general recognition that either you have "it" or you don't. If you are an inventor and are wondering whether or not you have "it," my best recommendation is to start networking (possibly through your local chamber of commerce) with business people in your area. Specifically look for those who started a business that was unusual, and especially look for those people who have started multiple businesses during their career. True entrepreneurs are in it for the challenge of building up the business. Once it's established, they tend to lose interest and move on. They are just as rare as the good inventor, and as sure as you should be looking for a good entrepreneur to help you with your ideas, they are looking for good inventors with good ideas that they can turn into new businesses.

As with my strict and contrasting definitions above for invention and product, I am going to be very clear in this book when I talk about people who might manage your product innovation business. Sometimes the functions are very appropriate for a well-trained and good-quality businessperson. Sometimes, the functions demand the skill and drive that you can only find in a true entrepreneur. In time, you will come to recognize the differences clearly. For now, just ask people that you meet: "are you an entrepreneur?" If they answer by telling you they have a degree from Harvard, they probably aren't. If they answer by very excitedly telling you about their most recent, new-business enterprise . . . they might be!

Leadership versus management. A big challenge in any business enterprise is providing effective management and leadership oversight to the organization. Any inventor will undoubtedly have an *ex officio* role in the management and/or leadership of the business enterprise. However, this person's precise title and the extent of his responsibilities are probably yet to be determined, and I will delve into these subjects in more depth in Chapter 7. For now, just accept that the inventor will be a prominent part of that team and that one of the inventor's key roles will be to ensure that the entire enterprise has proper leadership and management, which will involve more people than himself.

If you have worked in large organizations before or have spent time in the military or the Boy Scouts or the Girl Scouts, the subtle differences between leadership and management are probably not new to you. If you lack that kind of prior experience, then the words might seem to be somewhat redundant or synonymous. In this case, allow me to clarify the differences because there will be times when moving the project forward demands effective leadership, whereas at other times the required action is effective management.

Leaders lead people and managers manage projects. Said another way, people require effective *leadership* in order for them to work together toward a common objective. Whereas projects require effective *management* in order for them to be completed successfully and achieve their stated goals for the organization.

I believe that an effective manager can learn much of what is necessary to manage programs by studying the standard practices of business management and gaining first-hand experience with managing programs. On the other hand, effective leadership comes from a combination of personality traits that, for the most part, are instinctive to a person rather than learned outright. You have heard the phrase "born leader," right? That said, I couldn't recall anyone ever saying that a particular person was a "born manager!"

Good leaders tend to be "people magnets" and charismatic. They tend to see through clouds of confusion and be capable of plotting a course forward regardless of uncertainty. They are highly confident, and breed confidence in other people. Most important, they are driven to see others succeed more so than themselves. In short, effective leadership is what it takes to transform a collection of talented people into a well-connected group of co-workers who have a common goal and sense of *esprit de corps* and who can collectively solve hard problems and move a product-development effort forward.

Good managers tend to be fact-and-figure people who usually work just as effectively by themselves as they are able to work in a group. They tend to take a cloud of confusing information and organize it in a way that allows them to see trends and predict outcomes. They are also highly confident and generally instill that same confidence in others through their track record of proven performance in bringing projects in on time and on budget. In short, effective management is what it takes for any business to transfer a product-development plan on a piece of paper to an actual product in real life.

Just as in the case of entrepreneurs and businesspeople, you will find that your business enterprise needs both good leadership and good management in order for it to be successful. However, don't think that all good entrepreneurs make good leaders or that all good businesspeople make good program managers. The functions are different. Sometimes you find the rare individual who possesses all skills. More often than not, you find key people who are good in one or two areas, and you find others who have the complimentary skills. Ultimately, regardless of whether your management corps consists of one or ten people, it must possess the right combination of entrepreneurial drive, business savvy, leadership skills, and management expertise, if you are to be successful.

Strategic versus tactical. In setting up a product innovation business for success, and ultimately in managing the business on a day-to-day basis, there is an on-going challenge to split one's focus between the "what-ifs" of the distant future and the "oh-shits" of the immediate present. If you haven't yet launched your business, then you are mainly thinking about the "what-ifs" – the myriad of possible scenarios that your business might encounter and the range of possible fates that lie ahead. If you just launched your business recently, then you are almost certainly absorbed in dealing with the inevitable "oh-shits" – the unavoidable and unpredictable problems and challenges of daily life in small business.

> Considering the "what-ifs" is a *strategic* planning exercise – an exercise of your ability to create a distant vision for the company and your product that positions you for commercial success. Dealing with the daily "oh-shits" is a *tactical* execution exercise – an exercise of your ability to react and respond to the immediate, and often unanticipated, problems that are encountered.

To be successful, your business needs to be able to engage in both strategic planning and tactical execution. To be REALLY successful, you need to be great at both and ensure that both activities inspire and motivate each other constantly and purposefully. In choosing the right action to take in light of today's crisis you must be able to raise yourself out of the panic mode of the moment, and base your decisions on some consideration of the effects these actions will have in the context of the company's strategic plan and vision. Similarly, in establishing a strategic plan and vision, you must be fully aware of the details and complexities of tactical life. A strategic plan that cannot be reduced to a series of tactically executable steps is worthless!

Much of this book is written at a strategic level, which is to say that the concepts and recommendations discussed here are mainly useful to you as you take the distant view of your company and as you begin the process of developing your strategic plan. However, I am personally very driven to talk at the level of execution (rather than *keeping my finger nails clean* in an all-day strategic-planning session!). Indeed, I fully appreciate the critical importance of tactical execution to all businesses, and probably expend at least half of my consulting efforts in solving my clients' tactical problems with the remaining half of my efforts addressing strategic issues.

So within this book I will frequently expand on discussions of strategic topics by giving specific examples that demonstrate how such concepts can be worked into tactically executable plans. I will also provide references periodically that will give more detail on tactical issues than what I have space to discuss. Ultimately, as I will discuss in the final chapter of the book, I believe strongly that in order for you to be successful with your business you and your team of leaders and managers MUST be able to see the future reasonably clearly in the form of a strategic plan and vision. However, in order for you to actually move forward and realize that vision, your team MUST also be adept in the art and science of tactical execution.

Creative thinking versus structured thinking. In the study of modern psychology, you will find references to *right-brain behavior* and the *left-brain behavior*.[11] This distinction has been struck, not as a geometric demarcation, but as a means of dividing thought processes and categorizing personality traits and preferences. In short, it is said that people who are *left-brain-dominant* tend to be more structured and method-driven, which is to say that they think in step-wise fashion and tend to organize information in a spreadsheet sort of a way. Conversely, people who are *right-brain-dominant* tend to think more amorphously – without the aid of structure and obvious organization. Indeed, right-brain-dominant people tend to prefer disorder and revel in the freedom of such a thought environment.

Engineers are classically seen as left-brain-dominant people, whereas artists are classically seen as right-brain-dominant people. So which side of the brain drives invention? I suspect that this question could trigger quite a debate (and possibly many proposals for government-funded research grants) among the psychology community. Without the "burden" of years of formal education in the science of psychology, I would argue that to invent and reduce an invention to practice demands both the right and left sides of the brain.

---

[11] http://www.web-us.com/brain/LRBrain.html

Most likely, the moment of conception of a new idea is a moment of right-brain-dominant thought. It is an instant when out of nothing is derived something. Almost by definition, this pre-invention moment is without structure and form, as it is a collection of disparate thoughts and ideas related to a given topic, but lacking a central idea (i.e., the *invention*) to tie them together. The actual moment of invention is an act of structuring those disparate thoughts into a collection that defines order.

So given this argument, I would further assert that, by inventing a new idea an inventor has demonstrated healthy activity in both the right and left halves of his brain! No need for further psychoanalysis, right? Despite what his family and close friends might be saying about his strange passions and long hours alone in that messy garage!

Kidding aside, I believe this distinction and balancing of thought processes is not only critical to the act of invention, but also to the process of creating a successful product out of that invention. Indeed, there will be many moments down the road when prudence dictates that the left (i.e., structured) side of your brain take the controls and lead your actions following a very methodical and possibly well-defined process. But just as surely there will be moments that, in order to see a path forward, you will have to throw out convention and structure and focus the creative engine of the right half of your brain in order to see a pathway that is non-obvious or "invent" a new approach to deal with certain problems.

Overcoming challenges in product innovation business requires that you know and become comfortable with the concept that only certain challenges require creative solutions whereas others simply demand the application of existing and well-structured solutions. Don't hesitate to create when necessary, but don't ignore the vast body of existing experience in this business sector, as it will make your life much easier if you apply it effectively.

Have you ever felt like you had a mental block at work or possibly at home when you were trying to do something new? We all do, and we often find that the best means to break the block is to drop the issue for the time being and take a walk to clear our heads. Well, given the concept of right-brain/left-brain thought process, it is possible that the mental block is a result of looking at the problem with the wrong side of your brain! Furthermore, to clear the blockage just requires that you give yourself the opportunity to reassess the issue from the other, or maybe both, sides of your brain! (Again, here's a great topic for Federal research-grant funding!)

In my view, mastery of the business side of invention starts with a very basic recognition that different decisions and actions demand different mental approaches. Sometimes you will quite literally feel like you have to invent something new in order to move forward. If so, approach it as you would approach the creation of any invention – start on the unstructured side and move towards structure. However you must also recognize that many problems that you will face are classical problems of business, with the solutions of these problems readily available to someone who may simply be more versed in the world of business. It is in these moments that you can *and should* seek the guidance and help of outsiders with those experiences rather than to reinvent a solution for the pure joy of invention. Don't worry. There will be plenty of joyful moments of creation to satisfy that urge in you without reinventing the world of product innovation businesses!

Summary

To a much greater extent than most other types of business, product innovation businesses demand a very unintuitive balance between opposing forces. Creativity and entrepreneurship beget the new idea and conceive of the new market opportunity around that idea, while the disciplined application of classical business management and engineering principles are essential to mature the idea to a commercially viable product. At the center of the enterprise will be the inventor whose passion and inspiration is critical at the moment the idea is conceived and can provide many advantages to the enterprise if she is willing to give up a certain amount of control and ownership to others who will be critical allies in her enterprise.

Where is the common ground? For one thing, optimism and a pure sense of joy in learning new things are absolutely essential qualities for both inventors and entrepreneurs. If you are an inventor and you can find joy in the explorations and discoveries that are necessary to refine your invention and bring it to the market, you can be certain that the path ahead will be fun and fruitful. If you are an entrepreneur or other stakeholder in the enterprise and you can learn to appreciate the joy of discovery that drives the inventor to invent, you will find common ground in the shared experience of joy that accompanies the myriad of discoveries yet to be made on the business side as the enterprise grows and thrives. Either way, taking the journey will be as satisfying as reaching the destination, if you can find joy in the 99% worth of perspiration that is inherent in product innovation business.

Recently, I attended a workshop on small product innovation businesses where one of the speakers – a very successful entrepreneur and inventor – brought it all into clear focus for me with a simple and personal admission. He said that the reason that he was successful in product innovation business is the very same reason that he was creative with his inventions. In both cases, he said: "it's like solving a puzzle, and I LOVE puzzles." If you hate puzzles, this is your last chance to put the book down and walk away – again, I take no offense and respect your honesty! But if you love puzzles, and want to build a product innovation business, then get ready for the most important puzzle of your career – *The Inventor's Puzzle.*

2

A 600-Year-Old Template for How to Succeed in Product Innovation

"Never before in history has innovation offered promise of so much to so many in so short a time."

– Bill Gates

Small, product innovation business is the domain of genius, passion, and oftentimes frustration. If it is the womb of innovation for the technical elite, it is also their kindergarten where education in business begins. The breadth of challenges placed on these inventors and aspiring small-business leaders is expansive and daunting. But if these challenges are approached with the same discipline, vision, and determination that are applied in solving technical problems, the inevitable business challenges are just as solvable and the successes that are achieved in the board room can be even more satisfying than those that are achieved in the laboratory.

This chapter is intended to be a first exploration of *The Inventor's Puzzle* and a first lesson in the study of how to address the challenges of product innovation business. It will illustrate broadly five puzzle pieces – the technical problems and business problems that are systemic in product innovation businesses – and the interconnections between these pieces. It will further explore the "yin and the yang" of technical and business issues identified in the previous chapter, and further shed light on the elements of management and leadership that are essential: certain elements that are instinctive and natural to all engineers, scientists, and inventors, and some that are very unnatural and unintuitive.

Rather than being a blunt exposé derived from a mass of business school course notes, this chapter is a more subtle and thought-provoking view of the problem told using a real life example from the time of the Renaissance. The business-success story that is explored is the construction of the great dome of the cathedral of Santa Maria del Fiore in Florence, Italy during the 15th century. The inventor and entrepreneur who is explored is Filippo Brunelleschi (pronounced like *Broonl-eskee*). In overseeing the construction of the dome, Brunelleschi essentially created a template for success in product innovation businesses that is just as relevant today as it was 600 years ago.

To be successful, Brunelleschi not only had to invent numerous mechanical devices and methods in order to build the dome, but he also had to invent many very important business concepts like intellectual property strategy and protection, engineering methods, organizational management, strategic and tactical partnerships. I have chosen his example to expose the challenges of product innovation businesses because inventors will immediately identify with Brunelleschi, the archetypical inventor, and non-inventors will identify with Brunelleschi, the archetypical product innovation businessman.

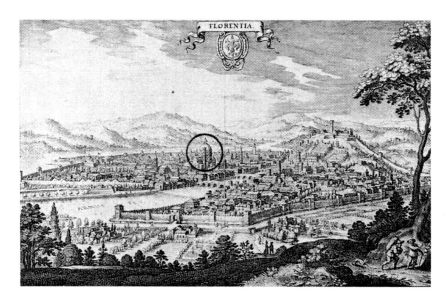

A 1650 lithograph of Florence ("Florentia" in Latin) drawn by Matteo Merian and showing Brunelleschi's Dome towering over the skyline.

In explaining proper modern day business practices in this way, I am intentionally discussing the problem from a distinctly different perspective than you might get in a run-of-the-mill business school curriculum. This is not meant to disregard modern day norms for teaching good business practices. Indeed, I will spend the next five chapters talking about these modern day norms. Rather, I am trying to speak from the clean slate perspective that Brunelleschi had 600 years ago without any formal training in the business world. Indeed, the very perspective that you might currently share if you have no experience in building a successful product innovation business. In this way, I hope that the basic concepts essential to your business success will settle into your mind in a more intuitive and perhaps commonsense way.

Filippo Brunelleschi – the archetypical inventor and product innovation business leader

So let's begin by getting to know Filippo Brunelleschi (1377 – 1446) himself.[12] Brunelleschi was a native of Florence, Italy, and became one of the most influential architects of the Italian Renaissance. Brunelleschi's work spanned several decades and demonstrated his mastery of a wide range of artistic and technical skills including sculpture, painting, metal work, and masonry construction. Above all other accomplishments, Brunelleschi is known for his work on the construction of the Dome of Santa Maria del Fiore. It was this commission that ultimately consumed most of his adult life, focused his immense technical and creative skills, and forced him to invent not just successful mechanical devices and methods, but also successful business practices.

Brunelleschi might be contrasted with a much more famous Italian inventor born two years after Brunelleschi's death in the little town of Vinci about 20 miles away from Brunelleschi's home in Florence. Leonardo da Vinci is often considered to be the quintessential artist and thinker of the Renaissance. Indeed, his very name has become synonymous with the Renaissance movement in Florence. However in my view, Leonardo was no Filippo Brunelleschi! Now don't get me

---

[12] *Brunelleschi's Dome: How a Renaissance Genius Reinvented Architecture,* by Ross King, Penguin Publishing (2001)

wrong; I absolutely revere Leonardo. But the harsh truth of the matter is that Leonardo thought of things that might one day be made practical by other people (e.g., airplanes, helicopters, parachutes, etc.), whereas Brunelleschi thought of things that he reduced to practice in his own lifetime.

In Chapter 1, I described two different types of creative people: people who create for the pure joy of it, and people who create for both the joy and the utility of it. Brunelleschi was an inventor for the practical reason that to be successful in his business as an architect he had to invent new things. A very early account of Brunelleschi's life was written by Giorgio Vasari and includes the following description of his capacity to succeed despite adversity.[13] This description is offered as motivation for the modern day inventor and product innovation businessperson.

"Many are cruelly bestowed by nature with deformed bodies and repugnant features, but have souls of unequalled greatness and courageous hearts, so that they find no peace in life unless they meet great challenges and achieve hugely difficult deeds, and when fate delivers base and vile things into their hands they are able to transform them into wonders."[13]

At a time when there existed no professional titles like CEO, COO, CTO, and CFO, Brunelleschi bore essentially all of these responsibilities under the title of *Capomaestro* – Master Builder. Furthermore, at a time when there were few formal laws and practices related to business structure and interactions, Brunelleschi created and managed large organizational units by instilling union-like practices and standards. He maintained a sprawling supply chain by establishing concise statements of need (i.e., contracts) and metrics of performance and payment. Finally, and central to his success, he effectively fended off many competitors through a very artful set of practices for the retention and protection of his ideas (i.e., his intellectual property). Brunelleschi's achievements in this area alone would justify an honorary doctorate degree from Harvard, post-humus of course!

---

[13] For an English version of Vasari's description of the life and work of Brunelleschi, see: [http://www.fordham.edu/halsall/basis/vasari/vasari5.htm]

It has been said that the world's first patent was granted to Brunelleschi in 1421. I will discuss Brunelleschi's patent later in this chapter and will discuss modern patents and government-granted monopolies in Chapter 4. At this point it is sufficient to point out that Brunelleschi might have invented the idea of patenting inventions, and was likely driven to do so by the very practical realization that he could make more money by maintaining a monopoly on his ideas.

Brunelleschi is quoted as having once said: *"Only the artist, not the fool discovers that which nature hides."*[13] This quote provides a bit of insight into how Brunelleschi saw himself in relation to others – including his competitors. In the time of the Renaissance, there was no proper word for "inventor." Instead, the process of invention was seen as an extension of the process of creating art – an extension that resulted in the application of artistic creations in solving real-world problems. I believe that Brunelleschi saw his work as all modern inventors should see their work – an answer to society's need to create things of beauty that actually serve a practical and valuable purpose. In possible contrast to Leonardo, Brunelleschi had great disdain for inventors who had no motive to reduce the invention to practice, or artisans who could do nothing but apply the practices that others had taught them.

As you move forward with your inventions and ideas make sure and pass them through a business "litmus test," as Brunelleschi might have done, in order to distinguish his work from the pretenders of his day. Ask yourself if your idea serves a practical need or is it just full of creativity and art. Herein is where you will find the true genius of your ideas, and if you see this genius it is very likely that you can get others to see the same! Now, let us explore the project that was Brunelleschi's puzzle – the construction of the dome of the cathedral of Santa Maria del Fiore.

Brunelleschi's dome – a short history

In 1296, the city of Florence Italy established an organization of local businessmen and wealthy land owners, the *Opera del Duomo* (the *Opera*), to oversee the design and construction of a cathedral – one that would rival the great gothic cathedrals in France, Germany, and England of the time. Aeroflot di Cambio developed an initial design for the cathedral in the Gothic style in 1296, and construction work began shortly thereafter. But in 1366, the *Opera*, following the advice of certain painters and sculptors, decided that the Gothic style should no longer be used and that all new work should follow Roman forms, including an octagonal dome 42 meters in span.

The *Opera* commissioned a second design study in 1366 from Neri di Fioravanti, the prominent Florentine architect who had designed the now-famous Ponte Vecchio Bridge in 1345. The goal of the study was to develop a design for the dome that would give it a novel appearance unlike the gothic cathedrals elsewhere in Europe. Neri di Fioravanti's solution was a self-supporting dome similar in concept to the Roman Pantheon, but distinctly different from the Gothic domes of the period, which gained their strength from external-supporting buttresses. The members of the *Opera* immediately accepted Neri's design as the final design, and from that date until the eventual completion of the cathedral, 70 years later, all members of the *Opera* took an annual vow to ensure that Neri's vision was realized in the final construction!

Physically, the dome was, and still is, the largest, freestanding masonry dome in the world. Its internal volume is large enough to enclose the entire dome of the U.S. Capitol building! Even today, it is the largest structure in the Florentine skyline, making it is easy to see why the members of the *Opera* enthusiastically accepted Neri's design in 1366 over the original plan and other less dramatic concepts that had been put forward.

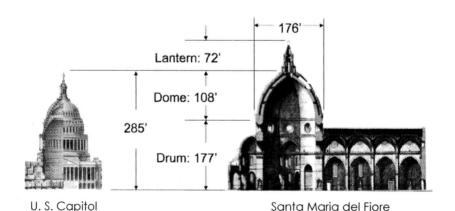

A comparison between the domes of Santa Maria del Fiore and the U.S. Capitol

For all of Neri's genius and creative skills, his design for the dome was far from complete. His design lacked the basic engineering elements like structural loads analysis, sizing and design of critical members to withstand such loads, and selection of proper materials. Most critically, Neri's design lacked a plan for how to build the dome without the aid of external bracing. As an engineer, it is almost incredible for me to recognize that the authoritative members of the *Opera* chose such a revolutionary design with blind faith that the details could be worked out and the dome could be built! (Apparently, 14th century government employees were about as responsible with taxpayer money as 21st century government employees are.)

Neri di Fioravanti was involved in the construction of the cathedral, including the early stages of construction of the *tambour* or *drum* – the lower chamber – of the dome, until his death in the late 1300's. The construction of this portion of the dome followed relatively standard practices for the period, and was completed in 1413. With Neri's death and no written documents to explain how to build the dome itself, the *Opera* had to ask for proposals from other architects for the design and construction of the dome in 1418.

Among the proposals was one from a local architect of modest fame, Filippo Brunelleschi. Brunelleschi's proposal was very distinct from all others in that he proposed to construct the dome using entirely freestanding construction techniques without the aid of any kind of temporary scaffolding or centering structures. Although his proposal was very compelling to the members of the *Opera*, Brunelleschi was very secretive about the details of his ideas and proposed methods. When challenged by the members of the *Opera* for clarification and explanation, he responded to the effect that his ideas were "clever, but quite straightforward, and once explained, they could be easily reproduced by any other architect."[13]

At this early stage in the competition, Brunelleschi understood that he lacked the strong reputation of other local architects, and if he was to be successful in winning the commission, he had to protect the thing that gave him advantage over that competition – his unique ideas. Somewhat reluctantly, the *Opera* awarded Brunelleschi a partial commission and the position of *Co-Capomaestro* (co-master builder) along with one of his archrivals, a local artist and would-be architect of great fame, Lorenzo Ghiberti.

This then, provides us the background to better appreciate Brunelleschi's astounding accomplishment. First, through his genius for architecture and construction, he saw a truly novel way to design and build the largest dome in the world without the use of external bracing. Second, through his insight into the *politics* of business, he recognized that his existing reputation alone was not sufficient to win him the most-coveted commission in Florence – he knew that he had to protect his novel ideas from piracy by the competition in order to succeed. Finally, through his own self-confidence and drive to succeed, he established a new reputation that ultimately gained him a position of pre-eminence, both in the eyes of the *Opera* and many other benefactors and customers of the time.

The first piece – know the customer and beat the competition

The customer in this story is the collection of authoritative members of the *Opera del Duomo* who had for the past 50 years taken an annual oath to see the dome of the cathedral built as Neri di Fioravante had envisioned it. Have you ever heard the classic frustrated salesperson's adage: "The customer is ALWAYS right"? Well, apparently this saying was true in 15th century Florence, because none of the architects of the day could persuade the *Opera* to reconsider such a revolutionary design for which no clear concepts existed for its construction! Such it was when the *Opera* opened the competition in 1418 for new proposals on the topic.

First and foremost, Brunelleschi not only believed that the customer was right in insisting on a novel design for the dome, but he was passionately motivated to provide such a novel design. Furthermore, few things might have driven Brunelleschi harder than a genuine sense of competition, and an absolute hatred for his competitors. As Brunelleschi rose through his career and built a reputation for excellence, genius, and hard work, he found himself repeatedly in direct competition with another Florentine – Lorenzo Ghiberti. Like Brunelleschi, Ghiberti was a metalworker and goldsmith by trade. Unlike Brunelleschi, Ghiberti had spent most of his early career growing a strong reputation among the Florentine aristocracy, and building a large business related to metal sculpture and art, not architecture.

In 1401, Brunelleschi had lost a metal-sculpture commission to Ghiberti. The commission was for the design and fabrication of a set of bronze doors for the Baptistry of Santa Maria del Fiore – a smaller building adjacent to the main cathedral. However, despite his strong reputation as an artist and metalworker, Ghiberti had no formal training in architecture and construction, and his proposal in response to the *Opera's* 1418 invitation was long on artistry and eloquence, but short on substance and details.

After a long debate and compromise, the *Opera* decided to employ both Brunelleschi and Ghiberti in, what proved to be, a dysfunctional, two-headed management team. This compromise is considered to be a reflection of the fact that nobody (except Brunelleschi himself) could see a clear plan for building the dome. As such, the *Opera* decided to minimize its risk and hire both Co-Capomaestri. The pair started their involvement in the construction in 1420, bickering and accusing one another of incompetence: the toughest, and the only really competent one, was Brunelleschi whose brilliant ideas, prior architectural commissions, working models, and commanding sense of optimism, slowly won him a position of favor in the eyes of the *Opera*.

The dome construction proceeded under this strange management arrangement for a period of about nine years during which the *Opera* progressively adopted Brunelleschi's ideas, while Ghiberti slowly saw his role (and salary) become subordinate to Brunelleschi. By the late 1420's when construction had proceeded to its most-critical phase – the vaulting of the Dome – Brunelleschi finally ascended to the full responsibility of Capomaestro with a further pay increase and a reinstatement of the $100K prize that he was never awarded after the original 1418 competition.

> Brunelleschi's ability to understand the customer and exceed the competition in the customer's eyes identifies the first issue that modern-day inventors and entrepreneurs must address in evolving an invention from concept to successful product.

As I mentioned in Chapter 1, the difference between an invention and a product is that an invention is an idea, but a product is an idea that someone will buy. Brunelleschi knew that to be successful he had to first understand what the customer wanted and what the competition was capable of providing (or incapable of providing, as the case may be!). Then, and only then, was he in a position to bring forward inventions that served a purpose and gained the customer's support.

Extending this concept one step further, in Chapter 3 I will discuss a modern-day archetypical example that illustrates how the market (i.e., the customer and the competition) for today's product innovation businesses is generally a moving target. This example is found in Apple Computer's 25-year push to innovate in the personal computing market with their Macintosh series of computers. Like Brunelleschi's attack on Ghiberti, Apple started their marketing push in 1984 by attacking and conquering a clearly defined element of the competition – IBM – with a product offering that addressed a critical need among the customer base – simplification of the operation of the personal computer through the use of a graphical user interface (GUI). Unlike Brunelleschi, Apple, and indeed most modern product innovation businesses, exists in a very dynamic and changing marketplace, which requires a constant shifting of strategy to address the emergence of new elements of competition from other product innovation companies like Microsoft®.

The second piece – protect your ideas

Brunelleschi started his professional career, not as an artist or architect, but as an *artisan* – a metalworker and goldsmith. With the encouragement of his father who was also a skilled artisan, Brunelleschi took up an early apprenticeship with a Florentine goldsmith and metalworker. Throughout his late adolescence and into his early adulthood, Brunelleschi worked hard to master his hands-on trade, and took advantage of all opportunities to learn about the business side of the trade.

While in his early twenties, Brunelleschi decided to leave Florence and move to Rome. At first, his goal might have been to establish his own metalwork business, but in time, it became clear that his aspirations were much loftier than to be a skilled laborer. Indeed, he became very absorbed with studying the architecture of ancient Rome, and unraveling mysteries as to how the ancients were able to build the massive structures that remain there today.

One building that was particularly interesting to Brunelleschi was the Pantheon. The Pantheon was built in Rome between about 20-120 BC, and is a circular, domed building constructed mainly of concrete and brick. The dome was the largest built until that time, measuring about 142 feet in diameter and rising to a height of 71 feet above its base or drum. The exact method of construction of the Pantheon has never been determined, and this riddle obviously consumed Brunelleschi during his period of stay in Rome.

Brunelleschi's time in Rome is illustrative of the attitudes and ideas that were emerging among the Italian artists and intellectuals of the day. Indeed, his time in Rome is coincident with the beginning of the time period that has become referred to as the *Renaissance* – the reawakening of ancient ideas and practices among the intellectual and artistic community. So his study of ancient Roman architecture and his application of lessons learned from that study represent examples of a broader movement to bring ancient technologies back into modern practice.

Within a growing community of *Renaissance men* like Brunelleschi, there was a growing awareness that one could build a profitable business by understanding and harnessing the secrets of the past. Brunelleschi and many of his contemporaries were from modest financial beginnings, and had been raised to expect nothing more out of a professional life than sufficient money to raise a small family. In practical terms, it is likely that we can find, among these *Renaissance men,* the first roots of the modern-day concept of *intellectual property* – creations of ones mind that have value, and over which the individual can exercise rights of ownership. Certainly, these men were motivated not just by an academic desire for knowledge, but also by a practical desire for a better position in society!

Years later, after he returned to Florence and was competing for the 1418 commission of the dome of Santa Maria del Fiore, Brunelleschi's practice of closely protecting his ideas became a matter of public concern and debate. As mentioned earlier, he chose to repel probing questions by the officials of the *Opera* regarding the details of his plan out of his keen awareness of the value of these ideas to both himself and his competition. Although his move is seen today as a sound business practice, at the time, it was considered to be insolent by the officials of the *Opera,* and it nearly led to his proposal being dismissed outright.

Fortunately, nobody else proposed clear solutions for the problem, so insolence aside, Brunelleschi earned a "seat at the table" as Co-Capomaestro.

> Brunelleschi found himself walking a tightrope on how much detail to expose related to his ideas in order to: 1) satisfy the critics and sponsors, while also 2) preventing piracy by the competition. This struggle is possibly the archetypical example of the struggle that every product innovation business makes daily as they work to gain acceptance (and market share) for their new ideas, while managing the omnipresent threat of piracy by more established competition.

Brunelleschi's answer to this struggle involved several actions – actions that today are commonly applied in very similar fashion by all successful product innovation businesses as a matter of course in their intellectual property protection strategy.

Protection of written documents and trade secrets. Even at a very early stage during his studies in Rome, it is clear that Brunelleschi appreciated the concept of protection of intellectual property. Along with an early colleague, Brunelleschi created a method for writing his technical notes in a code that was difficult, if not impossible, for others to decipher. For years, he studied Roman ruins, and reduced his observations to volumes of notebook entries, copiously recorded in a private language that only he, and presumably a few others, could interpret. Today, we have given Leonardo da Vinci the lion's share of credit for using codes to capture important information.[14] In fact, this practice predated Leonardo by at least one generation!

Ultimately, these measures that Brunelleschi took to protect his *trade secrets* – secrets that were key to maintaining a competitive edge in his trade – effectively prevented Ghiberti from ever gaining the insight to reproduce what Brunelleschi was doing. In one, very classic moment that developed between the two, Ghiberti was tasked with oversight of a key

---

[14] *The Da Vinci Code*, by Dan Brown, Random House Publishing (2003)

element of the construction while Brunelleschi was out of town visiting with some suppliers of materials for the project. Prior to leaving, Brunelleschi had given Ghiberti some of the information that was needed to oversee the project, but he left out key details that ultimately led to a minor catastrophe on the worksite. When he returned and with great ease corrected the problem, Brunelleschi had also succeeded in reducing Ghiberti to a fool in the eyes of the *Opera*, which led to both Ghiberti's demotion and Brunelleschi's promotion.

Protection of inventions through patenting. As Brunelleschi advanced his work on the dome, he came to realize that many of his ideas could not be protected by simply encoding them within notebooks. These ideas had to be reduced to practice and given out to workers in order for them to be applied in the construction of the dome. At the time of the Renaissance, there were no governing bodies that saw a need or reason to protect individuals' ideas through a *patent* – a government-granted monopoly. However, Brunelleschi saw that many of these ideas, which were rooted in solving the immediate problem of building the dome, could have broader application and therefore represented something that he should benefit from financially beyond just the commission for construction of the dome.

One such idea was for a method of transporting goods up and down the river Arno in support of his construction of the great dome. To solve this problem, Brunelleschi envisioned a machine that sat on a flat-keeled boat, which was to be towed by smaller boats. As he worked through his design, he saw it as one that could be useful in a wider array of river-commerce activities, and therefore he petitioned the Florentine government to grant him an exclusive right to use and market the idea to other businesses.

After substantial debate, Brunelleschi negotiated a 3-year monopoly, which is in contrast to the 20-year monopoly granted in current U.S. patents. Also in contrast to modern patents, Brunelleschi's patent is vague about the nature of the invention. This vagueness is a reflection of the immaturity of patent law, as well as the closeness of Brunelleschi's relationship with the Florentine authorities at the time, and their trust in the value of his genius.[15] This patent was potentially very valuable to

---

[15] From IP Review Online, [http://www.cpaglobal.com/ip-review-online/widgets/notes_quotes/]

Brunelleschi as it would force merchants who wanted to supply materials for the great dome project to pay royalties to Brunelleschi for the use of his device.

In Chapter 4, I will discuss intellectual property protection practices in modern product innovation businesses, and will highlight examples that illustrate how to, *and how not to,* construct and market your intellectual property portfolio. An example of what to do is found in the Intel® Corporation's vast array of patented micro-processing devices, trade secret know-how, and copyright-protected software and firmware that are collectively marketed and easily recognized under the trademarked wrapper of "Intel Inside"®. Just as Brunelleschi was able to use a diversity of protection strategies to ensure his own success, Intel® has thoughtfully constructed and effectively marketed a diversified intellectual property portfolio to separate themselves from a whole host of un-recognizable competitors in the market to provide invisible "stuff" to the microelectronics-device industry - quietly growing to mega-giant status as a component provider to these giant corporations and dominating a price-driven market with products that command top dollar in comparison to the competition!

The third piece – be methodical in engineering your ideas into practical products

Of all the roles that Brunelleschi had to play in seeing the Dome through to its completion, it is the role of chief engineer to which he seems to have been most naturally suited. Within this role, Brunelleschi had to develop the details of the design of the dome, techniques and tools for its manufacture, logistics for the supply of materials and parts, and oversight of the workers at the construction site. In a modern-day construction project, this role alone would consume the efforts of a talented chief engineer. From the period of 1420-1434, Brunelleschi had to execute these responsibilities at the same time that he was dealing with the challenges imposed by the customer (the *Opera*) and the competition (Ghiberti).

Brunelleschi's innate talent for the role of chief engineer is clear in the fact that no formal engineering practices existed at the time to guide his actions. Indeed, in the estimation of engineering professor Filippo

44

Salustri from Toronto's Ryerson University,[16] modern-day engineering design principles can be traced to Brunelleschi: "The way he designed the dome [started with] the basic steps of doing some concept design and feasibility studies. He [then] selected a concept, eventually came up with a detailed drawing of the entire dome, and then he broke the dome design apart. He developed part drawings, sent those to random manufacturers, and told them all, 'Don't ask me what this is for; you don't need to know.' [As with other areas of his intellectual property, Brunelleschi] was afraid less scrupulous people might try to beat him by putting up a similar dome on a building."

Brunelleschi's basic six-step design process consisted of 1) analyzing design requirements, 2) making a concept design and testing the concept with sub-scale models, 3) making a detailed design, 4) planning the manufacturing process, 5) manufacturing the parts, and 6) assembling the parts. This method may sound conventional to modern engineers, but in Salustri's view (and my view as well), Brunelleschi was the first person in history to adopt this methodical six-step process. Clearly, Brunelleschi appreciated that the final design for a complex structure like the Dome demanded iteration and perfection through sub-scale models and testing – a process that was enabled through several private commissions that will be discussed in the next subsection.

> Brunelleschi's success hinged not only on his creative ideas and ability to secure support for the development of those ideas. Ultimately, his success hinged on his ability to evolve and perfect relatively complex designs through a disciplined process that is commonly accepted as the standard engineering process today.

Could he have been successful otherwise? It is impossible to say with absolute certainty, but it is very reasonable to assert that the methodical process of design development he adopted reduced to a minimum – and possibly eliminated – his risk of failure for technical reasons.

---

[16] *Turn on the Light,* by Jean Thilmany, printed in ASME Mechanical Engineering Design (2004)

In Chapter 5, I will discuss how modern product innovation businesses apply a standardized engineering process to the evolution of new inventions into marketable products. Most companies involved in product innovation today oversee the progress of such programs at the executive-management or Board-of-Directors' level in a process that reflects the style by which the *Opera* oversaw Brunelleschi's work. In particular, leaders of a modern product innovation company would likely review the progress of a product-development program using a standardized template of development milestones and performance metrics that couple the engineering-development efforts with other related efforts like market research. Such a project is designed to move forward incrementally until the next major milestone is successfully completed. If something critical goes wrong at any point along the way, the oversight committee has the power to halt the project.

This modern day product innovation business practice is a result of the need by the company and its financial backers to manage and minimize the risk of failure in bringing new ideas into the market. 600 years ago, Brunelleschi applied the very same methodical approach in order to manage and minimize the risk of failure of his own ideas, as well as to minimize the risk that the substantial sums of money committed by the *Opera* to support the construction of the dome would not be wasted.

The fourth piece – you need money to make money

The next piece of Brunelleschi's puzzle is that of money, or more specifically, the money that was necessary for him to further develop his ideas and ultimately reduce them to practice. As I have mentioned previously, Brunelleschi was not a wealthy person in his early life. Although his artistic eye and substantial skills as a goldsmith could have easily earned him a reasonable income in such a trade, his focus on learning the technical skills necessary to be a world-class architect and engineer prevented him from ever building a stable income until much later in life. So consistently and until he was several years into his position overseeing the dome project, Brunelleschi had to find the means to supplement his income. These additional commissions served to pay for the development of his novel ideas from early concept to a point of practical implementation where a paying customer (the *Opera*) was willing to accept the risk for further funding.

If you are an inventor, you have doubtlessly stared the issue of money squarely in the face, and likely you have had, or are having, significant problems in finding money to move your ideas forward. So did Brunelleschi. In fact, this issue could easily have erased his name from the history books. However, through a very determined and practical approach to the problem, Brunelleschi was able to secure key bits of money to keep his efforts going forward at times when the main customer (the *Opera*) wasn't yet ready to pay the bills. Ultimately, this tenacity and creativity in securing funding to keep his ideas moving forward led him to receive great financial rewards for his ideas in the end.

Grants from benevolent supporters. The economics of business in Florence during the Renaissance were quite a bit different from modern day business economics in that companies were not publically owned (i.e., traded on a stock market), and private investors generally did not seek to increase their wealth through investments in business. This was a time when the wealthy stayed wealthy while the poor stayed poor, and there were few opportunities for either to cross over into the other's socio-economic world.

The one exception to this rule is found in the private benefactors of the artists and academics of the Renaissance, such as the famous Medici family of Florence – the family who was almost single-handedly responsible for allowing Leonardo da Vinci to spend his life following scientific and artistic pursuits. Unlike Leonardo, Brunelleschi did not enjoy guaranteed financial support from these people, and he had to work hard to secure what support he received.

Such benefactors tended to provide funds for pursuits that they had particular passion for – *pet projects* – not necessarily pursuits that could result in new business enterprises. In fact, such benefactors were already financially secure and happy with their aristocratic position in society and had no particular motivation to see their money be used to seed a new-business enterprise that might help someone else climb into the aristocracy. To the contrary, these benefactors wanted to see that their money was used to seed work that might bring out new ideas of a scientific nature, or create artwork that would grow Florence's reputation as a world leader in Renaissance art.

It is important to recognize that many of these benefactors were also officials of the *Opera*, and in that capacity had visibility into Brunelleschi's ideas and insight into his abilities and personal aspirations. While his relationship with these benefactors ultimately helped Brunelleschi secure his role as Capomaestro for the construction of the dome, his focus on solving problems with commercial value and his penchant for protecting his ideas from outside exposure might have prevented him from gaining consistent private support from the same benefactors for early development of his ideas.

Government contracts. Although uninterested in writing a "blank check" to Brunelleschi, the members of the *Opera* did provide him with a modest initial contract at the time of the 1418 competition for a detailed design and construction method for the dome. This early contract gave Brunelleschi the use of free labor and building materials for a period of two months, during which he was able to build a scale model of the dome – sufficiently large for the members of the *Opera* to walk inside it, and sufficiently detailed for him to flesh out some of his concepts in practice.

Also at the outset of the competition, the *Opera* promised a prize (equivalent to approximately $100K in modern day dollars) to the winner of the design competition. Certainly, this financial prize would have provided Brunelleschi with additional means to explore and refine his ideas in private, and before exposing them to the *Opera* for detailed scrutiny. Unfortunately, instead of selecting Brunelleschi's proposal outright and awarding him with the $100K prize immediately, they agreed to give him the lower-paying position mentioned earlier as Co-Capomaestro, with the thought that they would revisit his ideas later, after he had better developed them.

Contracts from "early adopters." The relative lack of financial support from a benefactor like the Medici family or the *Opera* could possibly have driven Brunelleschi to achieve a higher level of success than he might have without such financial concerns. As it turned out, the relative lack of early-phase money forced Brunelleschi to secure smaller commissions from private people though which he could test his ideas on a smaller scale while refining them with the benefit of feedback from paying customers and prior to presenting them to the *Opera* for inclusion in the plans for construction of the dome.

One such smaller commission came from an upper class Florentine businessman who was looking for a unique architectural feature for his home. Brunelleschi proposed to design and build a small dome, similar to the design for the Duomo, over a portion of this man's home, using techniques similar to those he had envisioned for the Duomo. Possibly in a move that was intended to establish his own position more prominently in Florentine society, the man accepted Brunelleschi's proposal, and awarded him with a commission that proved incredibly valuable to Brunelleschi's efforts to refine his ideas.

In the context of modern day, product innovation business, such a customer could be viewed as an "early adopter" – someone who is intrigued by your new technology and has the financial ability to purchase it.[17] By marketing your ideas directly to this smaller segment of the market, you (the inventor) gain the double advantage of getting early-stage money and early customer feedback with which you can refine your ideas prior to entering the larger, and oftentimes more conservative, market.

Using early-phase funding to secure the market. At the time that Brunelleschi received this smaller commission, he was plagued by a general sense of skepticism and conservatism on the part of the *Opera*. Unlike their ready acceptance of Neri di Fioravanti's original design for the dome – a move that demonstrated their *de facto* acceptance of Neri as a capable architect, the *Opera* had become suspicious of Brunelleschi's secretive nature and had chosen to move forward very slowly in accepting his ideas.

After successfully completing the smaller dome-construction commission for the upper class Florentine businessman, Brunelleschi had demonstrated the credibility of his ideas and had begun to create for himself a stronger reputation as a capable architect. Although his ideas were probably not yet accepted *carte blanche* as the ideas of Neri di Fioravante had been accepted 50 years previously, his successful

---

[17] *Crossing the Chasm: Marketing and Selling Technology Products to Mainstream Customers*, by Geoffrey A. Moore, Collins Business; Revised edition (2002)

completion of this smaller commission must have earned him a great deal of increased respect. This small commission, combined with other circumstances more central to the Duomo project, brought Brunelleschi a significant promotion, increased pay, and ultimately, eliminated his main source of competition – Lorenzo Ghiberti – his archrival and Co-Capomaestro on the dome project.

As I will discuss in detail in Chapter 6, this part of the story about Brunelleschi is particularly important, but somewhat elusive, to the modern inventor and product innovation entrepreneur.

> Almost without exception, capitalization becomes a limiting factor at some point along the path from invention to market-ready product. Like Brunelleschi, those who accept this as a potential limitation and who work diligently to secure financial resources to evolve their technology and better position them for the ultimate market opportunity, are most likely to succeed. Those who ignore this issue and fall in the trap of assuming they can be successful by *working hard* and without having the benefit of *working cash* are essentially doomed to failure.

The fifth piece – no business succeeds without a good team

The statistic related to the Dome of Santa Maria del Fiore, which I find to be most impressive, is that approximately 20,000 pounds of building materials were delivered to the building site and raised to an average height of 200 feet above the ground each and every day throughout its 15-year construction period! Although a single tractor-trailer truck and an overhead construction crane could easily handle this task today, 600 years ago this task was accomplished with nothing but manual labor and the power of oxen and horses. Hence, a very clever plan for the design and efficient delivery of the materials was critical to keeping the construction project on schedule.

Up until this point in the story, it would be natural for you to consider Brunelleschi to be a one-man show. Indeed, many of his accomplishments in developing his inventions, protecting those inventions, securing funding for his efforts, and evolving his designs are largely attributed to his own efforts and the efforts of a handful of protégés working under his close supervision. On the issue of ultimately putting his ideas into practice at the construction site however, Brunelleschi had to build a very extensive family of vendors and suppliers, an intricate transportation network for the delivery of supplies, and a well-trained and highly skilled workforce at the construction site who could, with minimal supervision, be responsible for effectively translating his ideas into practice.

In populating his family of vendors and suppliers, Brunelleschi took great pains to establish relationships with people he could trust. In a process that is an archetype for today's "Toyota Model" for supply-chain management,[18] Brunelleschi first met with potential suppliers, then, assuming his impression was positive, he would grant the particular supplier a modest contract to prove his performance. In time, he was able to establish a family of vendors and suppliers who responded well to his changing needs and consistently provided him with quality materials and services.

In building a transportation network, Brunelleschi played several roles. First, he built relationships with service providers like those he built with the vendors and material suppliers. Second, he provided new ideas to eliminate limitations in the transportation network like the invention discussed earlier for a river barge.

In response to the worksite logistics problem of raising 20,000 pounds of materials 200 feet high each day, Brunelleschi invented an ox-driven hoist that was capable of raising a 1,000-pound load, 200 feet in the air in only 13 minutes. For this invention, and the dramatic effect that it had on accelerating the rate at which work could proceed, the *Opera* elected to give Brunelleschi an additional royalty worth approximately $50K in modern day dollars. Along with this invention, Brunelleschi had work crews specially trained on the operation of the hoist, and established (with their support) safety procedures that prevented any deaths or serious injury throughout the 15-year period of its use!

Also in the interest of ensuring efficiency and safety in the work force, Brunelleschi installed a cantina about 100' above the ground to provide

---

[18] *Toyota's Supply Chain Management: A Strategic Approach to Toyota's Renowned System,* by Ananth Iyer, Sridhar Seshadr, and Roy Vasher, McGraw-Hill (2009)

the workers with food without requiring them to climb and descend many ladders. He also adopted a practice of watering down the workers' wine (yes, wine was the preferred drink during working hours in 15th-century Italy!) in order to minimize hazards due to drunkenness. Finally, he installed a network of safety nets below the areas of active construction to minimize the risk of falling. In total, these efforts had a dramatic and positive effect on both efficiency and worker safety, with only three deaths total recorded throughout the 15-year period of construction of the dome.

As I will discuss in Chapter 7, Brunelleschi appreciated a basic fact governing how best to turn one's ideas into reality, which many modern day inventors don't fully appreciate.

Although the typical inventor might be able to accomplish many things by herself, it is impossible for her to ultimately get her ideas into the market without the help of others. For some programs, the necessary team might be rather small. For a large project like the construction of the dome of Santa Maria del Fiore, the team would be extensive, and the establishment and maintenance of the team would be as much of a challenge to the inventor as the creation of her inventions.

Summary

I began this chapter with a very powerful quote from Bill Gates, which states that the opportunities for new ideas to percolate into new and lucrative products continues to grow and expand in time. As a businessperson, technologist, and "shade-tree" historian myself, I would similarly assert that the free-market society of today is the ultimate realization of the thought revolution that occurred 600 years ago during the Renaissance. Indeed, Filippo Brunelleschi – *a true Renaissance man* - was successful in his career by becoming an archetype for modern day inventors, intellectual-property strategists, marketing and sales experts, and chief engineers and operations managers.

In de-constructing his issues and accomplishments into five pieces of a puzzle, I hope that you can start to see the essence of the challenges that lie ahead for you in your own journey to commercialize your ideas. More importantly, I hope that this explicit breakdown of the issues into a manageably small set provides you with a certain degree of confidence and determination knowing that, to be successful, the only requirement is that you understand and anticipate a relatively small set of top-level issues and take appropriate action to address each and every one of them as they occur. In essence, the same issues that Brunelleschi faced 600 years ago and the actions that he took in dealing with these issues have been refined into commonsense standard practices that drive today's product innovation business world.

Today, you can visit Florence and climb a long staircase, which is buried within the dome of Santa Maria del Fiore, all the way to the top of the structure. You can touch the very bricks that Brunelleschi's crane lifted off the ground 600 years ago, and you can see the intricate patterns that he designed to interconnect the brickwork such that the dome could be built without temporary supports. You can emerge from the top onto the Dome's great lantern and view the expansive exterior of the dome against the beautiful Florentine skyline.

My wife and I did this in 2002 – our first stop during a two-week tour of Italy. Throughout the remainder of that day, and with the help of a few glasses of native Chianti, I was completely immersed in Brunelleschi's brilliance and moved to better appreciate the impact that he has had on the modern world of product innovation businesses. I hope that the discussion here has helped you get to know this "founding father" of modern business better and appreciate how his successes have helped set the stage for your own successes. Indeed, this short lesson in Renaissance history might even compel you to plan your own first-hand encounter with *Brunelleschi's puzzle* in Florence as a means to celebrate your own future product innovation business success story! If so I heartily recommend that you plan to stay for a while and savor your own successes with a healthy side dish of Tuscan cuisine and native Chianti!

This chapter was intended to help you understand the five basic pieces of *The Inventor's Puzzle*, and appreciate the inter-connections between them and the significance that they represent to a modern inventor and entrepreneur. The following five chapters address each of these issues in the context of modern business. They are designed to provide you with a deeper understanding of each puzzle piece and, more importantly, a clearer set of actions that you must take in addressing the issues to set up your own business enterprise for success. Hopefully, as I stated at the beginning of this book, you will come to see these pieces of the puzzle as intrinsic to the world of product innovation business, and come to see the actions that are prescribed to deal with the issues as common sense. If I am successful at instilling in you that level of insight, I am confident that you will be successful in applying the insight gained to ensure your own business success.

3

The Market: An Introduction to Customer and Competition Assessment

"Necessity is the Mother of invention."

−Plato

Have you ever watched the movie "Field of Dreams," with Kevin Costner? If not, it's a 1989 movie about a Midwestern farmer and an avid baseball fan (Costner) who builds a magical baseball diamond, which becomes a practice field for the ghosts of many long-dead and famous baseball players. I love baseball and love many baseball movies, but not "Field of Dreams." No offense to Mr. Costner, because my favorite baseball movie is his 1988 classic: "Bull Durham." However, despite its huge popularity, "Field of Dreams" doesn't sit well with me because of its naively optimistic theme: "If you build it, they will come."

After 25 years in engineering, innovation, product development, and small business development, I've learned that if you build it without first talking with *them* − the customer, you can be virtually certain that they will not come! A few people might come (e.g., you might sell a few units to friends and family), but without having a solid understanding of the customer base, you can be almost certain that the product won't sell well. In short, there might be fields of dreams in Hollywood, but for all practical purposes, they just don't exist on Wall Street.

If baseball movies from the late 1980's are obscure references for you, I am certain that you have heard the famous quote "Necessity is the Mother of invention." What you might not have known is that the quote is a translation from writings of the great Greek philosopher Plato and dates to around 400 BC, which makes a 30-year-old movie seem new, doesn't it? For all of its eloquence this short phrase is, sadly, a bit too short to be practical for the modern day inventor. Although *need* partially defines the value of an invention, in today's world of highly competitive product innovation businesses *greed* plays an equal, if not greater role in defining value!

> A classic pitfall encountered by new inventors and young entrepreneurs is to mistakenly assume that a substantial segment of the market will naturally feel the same level of passion and desire for their inventions or ideas as they do themselves.

I can't begin to count the number of times that I have talked with someone about a great new idea that is (in their mind) the best thing since sliced bread, only to find out after a little bit of careful market analysis that, unlike sliced bread, which we all eat on a daily basis, this new idea has about as much market potential as *diced* bread, which we only eat on Thanksgiving, and only then if you happen to like stuffing!

It is in this moment of marketing enlightenment that I usually become the bad guy for having to tell the inventor or young entrepreneur that they have just invented the product innovation equivalent to *turkey stuffing*. This is usually not an easy moment for either of us. It feels rather like telling a new parent that their two-week-old baby is ugly. It might be very true, but it isn't something that one takes great pleasure in doing.

As I discussed in Chapter 1, invention is driven by passion, and I admire and respect – almost revere – those among us who have the passion to invent. But good business is built on greed, plain and simple. Therefore, good inventions are things that make the inventors passionate AND the greedy business people rich! If Plato had lived in the 21st century, and had investments in the stock market, I think he would have come to this conclusion also and probably would have added another line to his now-famous quote!

The purpose of this chapter is to discuss the market for your invention. I will talk about two basic aspects of the market: 1) the *customer base* – the group of people who are most likely to buy your product, and 2) the *competition* – the group of people who are, or will be, trying to keep you from selling products to that customer base. By the end of this chapter, I hope that you will have become armed with some insights and ideas that will help you to get to know both the customer and the competition better, and ultimately position you to develop a product that will sell and create maximum value.

This discussion is market independent, but I will bring up some examples in specific markets to illustrate key concepts. My intentions here are not to make you an expert in market analysis, nor am I going to give you enough information for you to perform a thorough market analysis for your product. Rather, my intention is to identify the key bits of information to gather through a proper market analysis, which will ultimately help you determine: 1) whether or not your invention is marketable, 2) what attributes of your invention are most valuable, and hence need to be aggressively protected using the intellectual property strategies discussed in Chapter 4, and 3) what are the critical design requirements necessary to drive the engineering and product-development cycle to be discussed in Chapter 5.

Who **is the market?**

To someone unskilled in the business world, "the market" seems to refer to a thing – an inanimate object, or maybe a place, like the place that you buy your produce. In truth, "the market" is not a single place or thing, it is a collection of people and organizations – a very dynamic and living organism. Like a living organism, the market behaves in certain ways: sometimes very predictable ways, and other times (like the Stock Market collapse in 2008) in not-so-predictable ways. If the market was completely predictable, then anyone could make a lot of money – right? Well, it's not completely predictable, BUT there are many things about its behavior that are predictable. So two keys to your success are: 1) basing your decisions on a good understanding of the predictable aspects of the market, while 2) also allowing flexibility within your plans for the unpredictable aspects of the market.

> The first lesson you need to learn as you develop your marketing efforts is that the market is not a collection of *what*, but rather, it is a collection of *who*.

Furthermore, this collection of people are very approachable and many of them are incredibly easy to talk with and very willing to give you information that could be critical to your understanding of the market as a whole. In short, understanding the market is an exercise in understanding the people and organizations that comprise the market. There are two primary types of people and organizations within your market of interest: *customers* and *competitors*, and you need to develop the skills and drive to get to know both of these groups of people intimately.

Learning your competition

One of the first questions I like to ask inventors and small business people is: "who are your competitors?" Amazingly, about half of the time, these people tell me: "we have no competitors!" This is amazing because of the statistics of the situation. Of the three to four million new companies that are started in this country each year, I would estimate that less than 1% of them are creating novel markets where there are literally no existing competitors . . . AS OF YET. The remainder of the companies – indeed, essentially every company – have competitors. More importantly, all successful companies know their competition very well, and understand how they can beat the competition. Beating the competition is not a random act of luck; it is a thoughtful process of first understanding whom you are up against and second figuring out how to be better than them in key ways.

Assuming that you have created an invention for something new, then let me ask you the question: "Who are your competitors?" If you have invented a new recipe for a cola drink, then it's clear that your competition includes the Coca-Cola® Company. If you have invented a new back-rubbing device – a product that might not exist currently in the marketplace – then you might not have to compete initially against other companies with similar products, but your competition would probably include the national network of massage therapists who would prefer that people bring their sore backs in for treatment rather than administering treatments themselves.

> You can start to understand who the competition is by asking yourself: "What businesses will be adversely affected when I bring this product into market?"

Some elements of the competition are clear, as they represent the existing companies who are marketing products or services that are similar to yours. Other elements of the competition are less easy to determine, as they represent the parts of the market that could be affected by your product or services, and that will respond to the introduction of those products or services in a very competitive way.

If the *market* is an organism, then the *competition* is a disease that you are trying to beat with *your medicine* (your product). But the competition isn't just a garden-variety disease; it is more like a nasty virus that can adapt itself to a wide variety of treatments. In most cases of new inventions being brought into the market, the competition is well entrenched in the market and healthy enough to fight off the attacks made by new product entries. In short, understanding the competition is key to developing a product with strong enough advantages to beat the competitive product(s), and a market-entry strategy that will allow you to capture the market despite the push-back you will get from the competition. Now, let me share a powerful example to illustrate the importance of understanding the competition.

In early 1984 Apple introduced a revolutionary new product into the computer market – the Macintosh® computer. The product introduction was heralded by a now-famous, multi-million-dollar commercial that Apple ran during the broadcast of Super Bowl XVIII.[19] The commercial was a very theatrical interpretation of the market impact that was expected with the introduction of the new computer product. Apple's main perceived competition at the time in the small-computer market – IBM – was portrayed as "Big Brother" in a one-minute adaptation of George Orwell's famous novel.[20]

This commercial, and the introduction of the Macintosh® computer line, certainly revolutionized the personal-computing industry, and ultimately eroded "Big Brother's" (IBM's) stronghold on that developing market. However, it is critical to understand that Apple's main competitive threat ultimately came, not from other computer manufacturers like IBM, but from a software company: Microsoft®. Indeed, at the same time that Apple was focusing most of its attentions on other computer manufacturers they essentially ignored the threat from software development companies like Microsoft®. In Apple's eyes at the time, software companies were *collaborators* – organizations that could contribute to, and benefit from, their own success through the marketing of related products and services.

Now we, and Apple, understand clearly that Microsoft® saw Apple as a competitor for the market share they were growing for their DOS operating system. Astutely, Bill Gates anticipated how dramatically the graphical user interface style of the early Macintosh operating systems would revolutionize the market for operating systems, and how quickly that market change could put his small company out of business. With this market insight, Gates aggressively went forward with his own "Windows" operating system – ultimately reducing the Macintosh operating system to a small market share while making himself one of

---

[19] "Apple's '1984' Super Bowl Commercial Still Stands as Watershed Event," by Kevin Maney, USA Today Technology Columnist, 1/28/2004, [http://www.usatoday.com/tech/columnist/kevinmaney/2004-01-28-maney_x.htm]
[20] *Nineteen Eighty-Four (1984),* by George Orwell, Secker and Warburg Publishers, London, (1949)

the richest men in the world. Indeed, the market determined that the most valuable feature of the early Macintosh computers was NOT the computer itself, but rather the operating system.

So a critical early step in the process of marketing your invention is to learn who the competition is – both the companies who have similar products to sell, and the companies whose business will be adversely affected by your new product. For each competitor, you must understand what they are good at, and what they are not good at. In total, you must understand what you have to offer that the customer would want to buy and the *competition* can't easily provide. You can start the process of defining the competition by asking, as I said before, the basic question: what businesses will be adversely affected when I bring this product into the market? Let this exercise be very expansive and inclusive. Consider every possible scenario you can conceive of, and be truthful - be paranoid – about the possible sources and motivations for competition.

You can start defining the competition by Googling on the computer and in your own mind. Eventually, and in an effort to refine and sharpen your definition of the competition, you will need to become more "extroverted" in your search – talking with as many people who represent the competition as possible, in order for you to really assess their strengths and weaknesses. Most likely, you will come to find that there is more than one competitor for your product. Some competitors will be defensive (like IBM in the preceding example) in protecting existing products in the market that your product might displace, while other competitors will be offensive (like Microsoft® in the preceding example) in creating new products that can more effectively compete with your product, and hence steal some, or all, of the market share that you are trying to capture.

Amazingly, if you are careful in your tactics, you will find that you can have fairly probing discussions with the competition, during which you will gather important insights into their strengths and weaknesses. In the example of Apple and Microsoft®, it is well-known that Bill Gates first presented himself to Steven Jobs (CEO of Apple) as a software-development partner, and in doing so he was able to learn a lot more about the Apple operating system then he would have ever learned if Steven knew Bill was going to steal his market! In a similar way, you should look for non-threatening ways that you can present yourself to the potential competition in an effort to "get inside their tents," and better understand their strengths and weaknesses.

If this style of market research is difficult for you to consider doing yourself, you need to find a partner who understands your goals, and who has the wherewithal to probe the market on your behalf. "Sniffing" around for market information and insights into the competition is second nature for a skilled marketing and business development person. If your enterprise is too young and cash flow is still an issue, you can consider bringing a market-research person on with a combination of a reduced salary and some equity stake (i.e., "back-end" compensation). The investment could be critical to your success down the road.

One other approach that you might consider to augment your personal market research effort is to enlist the service of a paid, professional market research organization. You can find such organizations in any large metropolitan area, and they can identify opportunities that you might miss, while independently validating the information that you might be able to compile on your own. Furthermore, a professional market research organization can give you a better feeling for how market statistics and critical market information should be efficiently summarized, which is a skill that you will need when you get to the point of asking people to invest in your enterprise (see Chapter 6).

In the end, you must create a reasonably accurate and comprehensive understanding of the competition in order for you to assess the marketability of your own product and develop a strategy for further development and launching of the product. Furthermore, you must always remind yourself that the competition – indeed the market – is dynamic and changing.

> You must not just create a "snapshot" of the competition that is unchanging in time. You must continually revisit your assessment of the competition, and look for changes in the market that could dramatically change the competitive landscape.

Apple finally figured it out (after firing and subsequently rehiring Steven Jobs), but it took them a couple of decades to regain the market advantages that they had in 1984 and the market share that established them as a giant in the microelectronics industry!

Learning your customers

At the same time that you are endeavoring to define your competition, you must also begin to define, more precisely, your *customer base* – the people who will actually buy your product. Just as with the competition, you will usually find that the customer base is not a single group of people, but probably multiple groups of people that represent subdivisions of the customer base into elements referred to as *market segments*. Likely, each market segment has slightly different needs and "appetites" for your new products, which might require a different sales strategy and/or slightly different versions of your product in order to be successful. For now, let's just talk about the problem of understanding a single market segment. The same process that is outlined below can, and should, be applied to all market segments you identify for your product.

Indeed, a natural result of learning about your competition is that you will begin to understand the customer base. Once you know against whom you are competing, you just need to know to whom they sell their products and services! So assuming that you have defined your competition well, you probably have developed a general idea about the customer base, including some valuable demographic information (e.g., age, where they live, where they shop, how much they typically pay for goods and services, etc.).

Get Out and Talk. Beyond these statistical bits of information about the customer base, learning what the customer base wants in a new product absolutely demands face time with people who are potential customers. Most inventors are passionate, and can use their passion to catch people's attention and start a conversation about their ideas. But in making these connections with the customer base, it is critically important to remember two things: 1) ALWAYS converse with people, don't preach to them and listen to what they have to say so you can learn from their comments in order to refine your own perceptions about what is valuable in your idea, and 2) ONLY describe your invention in general terms, and be sure not to give away ideas that are critical to making the invention work (remember Brunelleschi's lesson of protecting your ideas from being stolen by the competition).

In the next chapter, I will discuss the matter of intellectual property protection in great detail. At this point in the process, it is sufficient for you to know that there might be many attributes of your invention that are valuable to you. So as you talk with potential customers about your invention, just remember that a customer could become a competitor. Make sure and protect yourself from piracy in these discussions by not discussing product details with people who might become a potential competitor.

Most of all though, get out and talk! One very effective way of starting a discussion with a potential customer is to ask specific questions like: "What would you change about existing products?", or: "What do you not like about the current products in this area?", or: "Tell me your top two problems that the current products DON'T address." It is amazing how most people are very willing to talk about their problems. You can capitalize on this. Be anxious to hear what they have to say, and learn how to respond to their problem by describing how your invention will solve that problem.

Of course, you don't want to be a therapist; you want to be a successful businessperson. So what kind of information are you trying to gather when you talk with potential customers? You need to know anything and everything that will help you figure out if your invention will sell and how to sell your invention. Ultimately, you will know that you have adequately explored the customer base when you can answer the following questions:

What to Learn from Your Customers

1. Will my invention sell?
2. What attributes of this invention are most valuable (i.e., what does the customer need)?
3. How valuable are these attributes (i.e., how much of a premium will a customer pay for a more capable product like I am offering)?

Defining the business opportunity – "back-of-the-envelope" market analysis

At this point in the process, you should have a pretty good understanding of who the competition is and who the customers are. Hopefully, you have emerged through this process with a clear understanding that your invention will sell, and exactly what features it has (or needs to have) in order for it to sell. Now, it is possible to merge these pieces of information into a top-level market analysis that summarizes the business opportunity that you, and your prospective partners, are facing in *dollars and sense* – common sense, that is!

For it to be useful to you and your prospective business partners, this top-level analysis is simple enough that you can write it on the back of an envelope – figuratively speaking. Specifically, it needs to be concise and define only the *rough-order-of-magnitude* – accurate to within a factor of ten – estimate for the market size, and the number of products per year that your business might sell. It also needs to define a fairly accurate prediction (to within 20-40%) for the selling price for the product – the price that the market will bear, not the price that you wish it would sell for! Finally, it needs to define clearly the need(s) that your product is addressing in the chosen market segment(s).

How do you get these numbers? If you have done your market research well and taken good notes while you have talked with customers and competitors, you have gathered a combination of qualitative and quantitative data about the market. The *quantitative data* includes numerical information that defines the current status, and growth potential (in the case of a growth market) of the market – number of competitive products, average price of the products, size of the competitive companies, etc. The *qualitative data* includes non-numerical information that you have gathered that sheds light on the *appetite* of the market – the willingness of the market to accept new products. Developing your back-of-the-envelop market analysis is an exercise in merging these bits of quantitative and qualitative data, and answering the basic question of "how do I expect the market to respond to this product?"

Most business people tend to think of existing businesses in terms of the order of magnitude of their annual revenue stream. In other words, a business that has a stable revenue stream of $10M/year through sales of products and services is considered to be a $10M business (roughly speaking). Similarly, a new business opportunity is typically characterized by the business's potential revenue stream in the first several years (e.g., starting at $10M in the first year and growing to $50M over five years).

> A useful back-of-the-envelope market analysis needs to capture the potential revenue stream of the enterprise, represent a very reasonable estimation of the size of the business that you can create around your invention, and provide an outline for how potential investors will be paid off from this revenue stream.

With such a preliminary market analysis, your path forward will be much clearer than it was previously. Without it, (or with erroneous estimates) you risk moving forward in an uncertain direction and exposure to numerous potential failure scenarios.

In the end, a back-of-the-envelope market analysis is not only important for you in creating a strategic plan for your young enterprise, but it is important to attract additional financial resources (Chapter 6) and the interest of other top-level people (Chapter 7) who might help expand your enterprise. Indeed, one of the first questions you will get from a CEO candidate or a potential private investor will be "can I see your market analysis?" They want to know that your idea presents a good business opportunity at the outset. Remember, *necessity is the mother of invention, but GREED is its father!* And by the way, if you've padded the market-analysis numbers to feed your own ego, don't worry. The first time you share your analysis with a CEO candidate or a private investor, they will strip the padding right off . . . and possibly strip away a few layers of your ego in the process! So be as accurate and realistic in your market analysis as possible.

Revising the invention based on market needs

Hopefully you now have a realistic understanding of the market place and have gathered enough customer feedback that you understand better what your product has to do in order to be successful in the market. If you started this process thinking that your invention was complete at the moment of conception, by now you have earned a new perspective that the invention is not complete until the customer is happy with it! In Chapter 1 I told you that an "invention" is something new that nobody has thought of before. Whereas, a "product" is something that is either already in the marketplace or on its way to the marketplace, and that serves a specific need among the buying public.

If you have done a good job on your early study of the market, then you are in a good position to reassess your invention, and revise it in such a way as to better address the needs of the market. In order to walk you through the process of revising your design, I want to first introduce the concept of *engineering requirements*. This concept will be discussed in greater detail in Chapter 5, but I think the concept of engineering requirements is as critical to the marketing exercise as it is to the engineering-development exercise. Therefore, I believe it has to be an integral part of the discussion of both topics. In this section I don't want to explain engineering requirements rigorously, but rather summarize them from the perspective of the marketing department – the group of people who will ultimately be responsible for connecting you with the customer base.

All engineers are trained to recognize that in order to develop a design for a particular purpose it is necessary *a priori* to define what the device must do. This makes sense, right? More importantly, it is necessary to describe the functionality in precisely measurable terms, which are referred to as *requirements*. Otherwise, it is impossible to determine, with confidence, if the device that is ultimately built actually does what it was intended to do.

Now, this might sound a bit anal retentive to someone who has just created a new invention and built a working prototype in their garage. And, certainly, it is very possible to build things that work and that perform a function without ever taking the time to distill a precise set of requirements that describe this functionality. However, you absolutely must have such a set of requirements if you are to take this working model, and ultimately evolve it into a product that can be built: 1) in a repeatable fashion to a certain level of quality control, 2) at a certain price point, and 3) with the degree of designed-in functionality that is expected by the customer.

To illustrate why this level of rigor is necessary, I'll share the following cartoon that was drawn by a famous engineer-turned-cartoonist, Rube Goldberg. In it, you see a very elaborate invention that is built around a single engineering requirement – to build a device that makes it safer to walk on icy pavements. Of course, if you ever lived in the Midwest during the winter, the value of having a device that makes it safer to walk on icy pavements is clear! Unfortunately, this particular design might not be the best design. Even if it actually worked, could you imagine anyone buying it?

What if, before the engineering department went to work on their design, the marketing department imposed a few extra requirements on the design like: 1) the device must weigh no more than one pound in order for it to be easily carried, 2) the device must fit in a coat pocket in order for it to be conveniently stored when not in use, 3) the device must cost no more than $10 in order for it to be affordable by most people who might also buy umbrellas (i.e., a different product that is sold to a similar market segment), and 4) the device can't leave any dog poop on the sidewalk!. . . Clearly, meeting this expanded set of requirements would force the engineering department back to the drawing board!

At this point, you don't need to fully understand what would constitute a complete set of engineering requirements for your design. You just need to accept the fact that such a list must be created in order for your product-development effort to move forward. Furthermore, you need to recognize that the marketing department will have an equal stake, – no, a greater stake – in the creation of the requirements than the engineering department. At the end of the day, they want to know that the requirements reflect the needs of the customer, and it is in that way that they will, and MUST, be involved in the establishment of requirements.

> The requirements that are imposed by the marketing department represent a "mathematical" definition of the customer base – a measurable set of metrics that, if achieved in the design, should ensure that *if you build it, they will buy it!*

Once you have defined the customer's needs, it is essential that you take a fresh look at your invention and determine if it has all of the attributes required to make it successful in the market. Sometimes, your original idea will prove to be close to the mark. Other times, you will find that a thoughtful consideration of the real needs of the customer base point you in an entirely new direction – maybe leading to a major revision of your original invention, or the creation of an entirely new invention. Sometimes, you might find that there simply isn't a compelling need in the marketplace for your invention. If this proves to be the case, you absolutely must have the discipline to stop at this point. Or, at the very least, slow your activities down until such a time as you find another market segment that is in need of what you want to sell.

Preparing to sell yourself and your invention – the elevator pitch

Assuming that there is a market for your invention and you have absorbed enough insight into the customer base to understand how the invention needs to be evolved into a marketable product, you have made a critical step towards launching your enterprise. At this point, the business opportunity should be pretty clear. You should see, and be able to explain, not only if you build it they will buy it, but also how many they will buy each year and how much they will pay. This should be a very exciting moment, even more exciting that the moment when you first conceived of the invention. For, this is the moment when you first conceive of the business that will turn your invention into money!

Even though you are still quite early in the process, and have many issues yet to deal with (i.e., the subjects of the next four chapters!), it is not too early for you to start crafting and practicing the story that you will present to prospective business partners and investors who might become involved in your enterprise. You never know when you might meet someone who could be critically important to making your enterprise successful, and you should always be prepared to talk about your enterprise to such people in a way that will naturally attract their attention and build their interest in becoming involved.

This might sound like the easiest bit of advice that I've given you yet – talk to people about your passion, and get them interested! (As if you haven't already been doing that with anyone who would listen!) However, the kind of conversation I am talking about here is constructed in a very specific way, in order to quickly get to the point, and maximize your chance of leaving a positive impression on someone who could become critical to your success. This conversation is your *elevator pitch* – a top-level summary of your enterprise that you can give in the length of time it takes to ride in an elevator (maybe two minutes).

> The elevator pitch originated out of the simple recognition that the people who can be most critical to your success (e.g., financiers, strategic partners, advisors, etc.), are chronically busy and intolerant of mindless and wandering conversations.

These people who might be critical to your success simply don't have the time or patience to sit through a lengthy discussion on every issue and topic that you have considered since you first conceived of your invention – save the long talks for the next time you see your grandmother. Potential investors and business partners are only interested in the facts that are pertinent to defining the business opportunity, and they want those facts presented in clear and cohesive fashion.

If you do a Google search on "elevator pitch," you will unearth endless templates, lists of recommendations, sample videos, etc., that collectively define what this presentation needs to be like. Although there is no single, accepted format or outline, the following list of questions represents a good outline for constructing your pitch:

The Elevator Pitch

1. What is your product?

Describe the product you plan to make out of your invention. Keep it simple and focus on the attributes that will sell the product.

2. Who is your market?

Discuss to whom you are selling the product. How large is the market, how much of the market do you expect to be able to capture, and why?

3. Who is your competition?

Discuss who they are and what they have accomplished. Identifying successful competition is an advantage in that this proves there is good business in this market. Saying you have no competition indicates you have no understanding of the market.

4. What is your competitive advantage?

Describe how your product is different and why you have an advantage over the competition. Clearly describe your intellectual property, and your strategy for protecting it.

5. What is your revenue model?

Describe all elements of your product cost, including manufacturing, marketing and sales, and overhead costs simply. Explain how you expect to make money, and how you expect to pay your investors.

6. Who are your key leaders and who is behind the company?

Tell a little about you and your team's background and achievements. If you have a strong advisory board, tell who they are and what they have accomplished in past businesses. Describe any other investments you have already secured.

If you are going to cover all of this information in two minutes, you only have about 20 seconds to answer each question! Now do you understand why I told you earlier that it was critically important for you to be able to summarize the market analysis on the back of an envelope? If this sounds difficult, I'm sorry but you'll have to get used to it.

> If you are going to succeed in drawing people into your enterprise, you absolutely must be able to communicate in very brief terms the key bits of information that will excite them about your enterprise.

I recognize that you may not yet have enough information to create a complete elevator pitch, but you do have enough information to get started. Furthermore, I will talk about your elevator pitch again in a later chapter after you have more information with which to construct one. In the mean time, I personally think that it is good practice to condense your story into this format and take advantage of every opportunity to tell it, even at this early stage of your enterprise. You will be surprised how many people are interested in hearing your story, and how much additional insight you can gain about your early business plans through telling it. By the time you are ready to present the story to a real investor or CEO candidate, you will have refined and polished it to perfection!

Anticipating the shift from strategic to tactical marketing

Before leaving the discussion of market assessment, I want to touch on another dimension to this piece of the puzzle – the difference between market assessment and the action of marketing your business and product. Essentially everything that I have discussed in this chapter has related to the challenge of market assessment – determining the market and business opportunity for your invention. This type of marketing work is *strategic* in that it is helping you develop your long-term strategy for building your enterprise, developing your product, and ultimately entering it into the market.

Once you are moving forward with the enterprise, and are engaged in a product-development program, it will be essential for your organization to shift from *strategic* market assessment to *tactical* marketing and sales. In essence, the focus of the marketing department will shift from the long-term visionary work that is necessary to get the enterprise rolling, towards the near-term activities that will develop the market interest and convert that interest into product sales, which are necessary for the enterprise to become successful.

The subject of tactical marketing and sales is beyond the scope of the present book. For now, just recognize that once your enterprise is up and running, you MUST address this subject by making sure that you have people who are skilled in marketing and sales on your team. Furthermore, you should anticipate that the people on your team, who might be very skilled in the area of strategic market assessment, might have no particular skills for the challenges of tactical marketing and product sales.

Summary

Hopefully, you now see why "need" and "greed" are the two basic ingredients of any good business opportunity. There must be a need for your product or else nobody will buy it. Of equal importance, there must be a revenue model for your enterprise that allows the greedy investors to make a healthy profit on their investment while allowing you and your business partners to reap substantial financial rewards for all of your hard work. The sooner you can identify the *needy*, and build a story that satisfies the *greedy*, the sooner you will be in a position to launch your enterprise.

As critical as the issue of market assessment is, you must also realize that seeing the need and satisfying the greed, by themselves, do not guarantee success. Addressing these issues is just the first piece of the puzzle. If you have this piece well in hand – you have a good sense that if you build it, they will buy it. Now, let's take a look at the second piece of the puzzle by asking the question: "If you build it, can you be sure that someone else won't steal it?"

4

Intellectual Property: An Introduction to Legal and Strategic Issues

"If nature has made any one thing less susceptible than all others of exclusive property, it is the action of the thinking power called an idea, which an individual may exclusively possess as long as he keeps it to himself; but the moment it is divulged, it forces itself into the possession of every one."

–Thomas Jefferson

Assuming that you have an idea for a product, and have done enough early market research to see that there is a true need and appetite in the market for this idea, the next question you must ask yourself is: "Am I the first, or only, person who has had this idea?"; and assuming this to be the case, "How do I prevent someone else from stealing my idea?" Seeking the answers to these questions drives us into the discussion of *intellectual property* – novel ideas and inventions that you might own and that are critical to building your business.

Unfortunately, few inventors and businesspeople truly understand the legal and strategic issues related to intellectual property. As such, many small businesses with good ideas fail to realize a reasonable value from those ideas. Piracy of their ideas is the most-obvious means of loss, but there are many other ways in which improper planning and management of intellectual property leads to business failure. In this chapter, I will explain the key legal issues about intellectual property that you must know in order to assess your own current position. Furthermore, I will describe the key considerations that come into play as you develop a strategy for capture, development, marketing, and sale of your intellectual property portfolio.

If you are confused about what intellectual property means to you at this point in time, don't worry – you should be. Intellectual property is a complex topic and involves many non-intuitive elements. So in order to make sense of this critical issue, I will be discussing it from several different perspectives throughout this chapter. With patience and a willingness to read (and possibly reread) the following sections, I am confident that you can gain the same appreciation for the topic as most successful small-business CEOs.

The chapter will start with a practical definition of intellectual property, followed by a brief historical summary of the development in key pieces of law that establish government controls over intellectual property. Then I will discuss, in some detail, the four main types of intellectual property that you might deal with: patents, trade secrets, copyrights, and trademarks. Finally, I will discuss how to develop a strategy for the protection, and ultimately licensing and/or sale of your intellectual property.

Definition of intellectual property

Like any other type of property, *intellectual property* is something (presumably of value) over which you can assert legal ownership rights. To contrast intellectual property with *real property* – such as a home, farm, or vacant lot – intellectual property does not have to take a physical form, and is not necessarily embodied in a single object; rather it is built around ideas. Also unlike real property, ownership of intellectual property is not granted through a single deed or title, but rather through a collection of written and implied statements like patents and trade secrets, which collectively define the extent and ownership of the property – the ideas. A practical definition of intellectual property is as follows:

Intellectual Property includes creations of the mind (i.e., intellectual) for which legal ownership rights have been established (i.e., property), and that represent a potential business interest because of inherent commercial value.

76

Just as a person who owns a house or a car can seek to sell or license the use of (i.e., rent) that object of physical property, one who owns intellectual property can seek to sell or license the use of that intellectual property. Ultimately, the most likely means by which you will realize the value of the ideas you have invented will be through licensure or sale of the intellectual property portfolio that defines those ideas. Hence, it is absolutely critical that you understand how to establish your ownership rights over this property, so that when it is time to sell you have something to sell!

A brief history of intellectual property law

In Chapter 2, you gained a bit of insight into the development of the basic concepts of intellectual property during the 15th and 16th centuries. By the late 18th century, amazingly little progress had been made on the creation of laws that would govern intellectual property. However, the very young United States of America was soon to challenge that global trend.

At the time that this country was founded it was well accepted that the emerging printing and publication industry owed its livelihood to exclusive rights over the reproduction of written works. In addition, other means of protection of intellectual property like patents were being hotly debated among the founding fathers. Consequently, the United States Constitution (1787) authorized legislation: "To promote the progress of science and useful arts, by securing for limited times to authors and inventors the exclusive right to their respective writings and discoveries."[21] This key constitutional provision is the cornerstone of an extensive network of Federal and state legislation that has since been developed to protect your rights to the ownership of your own ideas!

One of the earliest Federal laws related to intellectual property protection was the Patent Act of 1793. With the passage of this law, we became only the second country to grant patents (Great Britain being the other country at the time). Interestingly, although Filippo Brunelleschi was successful in getting the first patent granted to him in Florence in the early 15th century, Italy did not establish national patent legislation until the 19th century.

---

[21] Article 1, Section 8, U.S. Constitution

Two of the greatest minds in America at the time of the framing of the Constitution and the passage of the U.S. Patent Act, Thomas Jefferson and Benjamin Franklin, stood at nearly opposite extremes in their views of patent law. Both statesmen were famous for being inventors, and both had very personal stakes in the rights of ownership associated with their inventions. However, Franklin is well known to have believed that all inventions, and indeed his own inventions, should rightfully be for the general benefit of society. Whereas Jefferson ultimately adopted the view that, like real property, inventions should be protected through exclusive ownership rights that are granted to the inventor and protected by the Federal government.

Franklin lived his philosophy by giving all of his inventions (including the lightning rod) away to anyone who wanted to supply them to the masses. Jefferson, on the other hand, kept his inventions (including the dumbwaiter) mainly to himself throughout his life and while he pursued the passage of Federal laws, including the Patent Act of 1793, to protect his, and other inventors' ownership rights.

To patent, or not to patent? was the question debated by Jefferson and Franklin. Shown here are their renderings on the $2 and $100 bills.

Interestingly, by late in his life, Jefferson felt that the experiment over Federal protection of intellectual property through patents had failed despite his substantial efforts. The quote that is included at the beginning of this chapter was extracted from a personal letter he wrote to a friend in 1813, in which Jefferson basically said that he felt like the practice of patenting in this country had proven to be a worthless practice. In his view, Jefferson had not seen sufficient proof that Federal protection of intellectual property ownership rights had done anything to stimulate innovation and the commercial markets!

Fast-forward 200 years. Can you imagine our economy today without Federal protection of intellectual property rights like patenting, trademark, and trade secret protections? There would be no Microsoft®, no Coca-Cola®, . . . no Starbucks® for heaven's sake! Fortunately for you, me, and everyone else who might have a marketable idea, Thomas Jefferson had the foresight to anticipate the lure of the marketplace for inventors. Did he actually foresee that the marketplace would be where the idea of the *American Dream* would be born? I don't think we could say so but clearly he had the practical insight into human nature to realize that people with good and marketable ideas should enjoy the rights of ownership of those ideas, and furthermore the Federal government was the best agency to protect those rights on behalf of the people.

hmmmm . . . Maybe we should have put Jefferson on the $100 bill and Franklin on the $2 bill!

This history lesson has brought us to a very significant aspect of intellectual property law – the fact that ownership rights for this type of property are mainly established through Federal legislation.[22]

This is in stark contrast to ownership of real property, which is protected at the city or county level, and some personal property like cars, boats, etc, which is protected at the state level. In the case of intellectual property, *Big Brother* – the Federal government – is the main governing body that protects your ownership rights. Now do you feel a little better about paying your taxes?

There are four distinct categories of intellectual property that I would now like to discuss in more detail: patents, trade secrets, copyrights, and trademarks. Afterwards, I will discuss strategies for protecting and building value in your intellectual property including ideas for how best

---

[22] Additional protections for intellectual property ownership are established through state legislation and in *civil law* – the collection of lawsuits that are raised nationwide related to intellectual property, but even these state laws and civil torts are consistent with Federal legislation.

to *diversify* your intellectual property holdings through a thoughtful combination of patents, trade secrets, copyrights, and trademarks.

Patents

Patents are probably the most obvious and best understood type of intellectual property. If you haven't already read a patent (or possibly applied for one yourself), you can download as many as you like at the U.S. Patent and Trademark Office (USPTO) website.[23] At the time of Jefferson and Franklin, the only mechanism for Federal protection of intellectual property was the patent. Since that time, the three other means of intellectual property protection, to be discussed in subsequent sections, have found their way into various pieces of Federal legislation.

Legal and strategic aspects of patents. By definition, a patent is a government-granted *monopoly* over an *openly disclosed* idea or invention. The process of filing for and gaining a grant for a patent requires the owner to fully disclose or describe the idea in sufficient detail that "someone who is skilled in the art could reduce it to practice."[23] Why then would someone choose to patent his or her idea? Wouldn't this immediately "tip your hand" to the competition, and cause you to lose valuable market advantage?

> Deciding to patent an invention is a decision to make that idea known to anyone who cares to know about it.

Well, there are certainly risks associated with any open disclosure of your ideas. That said the main strategic motivation to patent an idea is to gain the advantage of a government-granted monopoly for the use of that idea in the marketplace. In principle, the risk of loss of your idea to the competition is eliminated when you patent it. With a patent, the Federal government grants you the exclusive rights to the ownership and

---

[23] www.uspto.gov

use of that idea for 20 years. It is in this sense that a patent is, by definition, a government-granted monopoly.

Ever thought of it that way? Maybe not, but that is exactly what you get when you are granted a patent – that and an electronic copy of the patent filed on the USPTO website! Concern about government-granted monopolies is exactly the issue that Jefferson, Franklin, and others were debating in the late 18th century. When you think of a patent as a monopoly, then it is easier to appreciate why this was a hotbed of discussion 200 years ago. You can also appreciate the intense discussions that Filippo Brunelleschi undoubtedly had with the Florentine officials in the early 15th century over his petition for such government protection.

Most people appreciate why our government generally works to avoid monopolies - because they can be damaging to the marketplace. Indeed, our congress passed a series of landmark anti-trust laws in the late 19th and early 20th centuries in an effort to restore fair competition to the industrial sector of our economy, which had become dominated by a few very rich business giants like Andrew Carnegie and John D. Rockefeller. But in the case of new and emerging market segments, time has proven that an intellectual property monopoly can be a powerful stimulant for the marketplace. Indeed, patents are one of the leading reasons why this country has undergone dramatic, market-led technological revolutions over the years – from the industrial age of the 19th century to the explosion of microelectronics in "Silicon Valley" in the late 20th century.

Anatomy of a patent. If you have never read a patent, I encourage you to go to the USPTO website[23] and download a patent – any patent will do, but try to find one that is no more than 7-8 pages long, otherwise you will fall asleep halfway through the assignment! I suggest you read a sample patent in order to familiarize yourself with the general format of a patent. As you will see, the patent is divided into several sections, and includes numerous drawings (typically simple line drawings) to illustrate the invention.[24]

---

[24] If you want to learn more about how to read and interpret patents you can find several resources on the Web (e.g., http://www.bpmlegal.com/howtopat.html, http://www.patentlens.net/daisy/patentlens/ip.html). Shop wisely, as some of these on-line learning resources might cost a little money but many are free.

Did you read a patent? Are you familiar with the basic structure and outline of a patent? If so you can throw away all but the last page or two – the pages that list the "Claims." Indeed, this list is called "Claims" because this list is what the owner *claims* to own!

> In practical terms, all of the stuff leading up to the "Claims" is background material, and does not describe the property that is the subject of the patent. The "Claims" are the list of attributes of the invention, which together define the invention and the limits of the Federally granted monopoly on ownership.

I am amazed at how many intelligent, but ignorant, people have fallen prey to the misperception that the pictures included in a patent define the property that is owned! In fact, the pictures are there to illustrate the claims, but they do not establish ownership. Oftentimes, the pictures imply that the inventor has invented a fairly substantial thing, when – after thoughtful review of the claims – it is clear that the invention covers only certain elements or features of that thing.

Filing for a patent. So what is required to get a patent? Theoretically, the only requirements are a good idea that nobody else has previously come up with and a modest filing fee (around $300). In practice, the process of applying for, and ultimately getting a patent granted has become a bit tedious, and really demands the attention and counsel of a well-qualified intellectual property attorney. As such, the total cost for filing a patent application and responding to questions and challenges from the USPTO examiner can be $10,000 or greater.

It can and should take quite some time to hammer out proper claims. You should think about your patent claims with the same diligence that you would think about the survey of the property on which your house sits. You can build a fence, plant a shrub line, and do anything you like to give the appearance that your property extends further than it might actually extend, but the recorded survey in the County Clerk's office officially defines the property line, and is likely to be called into court if your neighbors think you've gone over the line! Such it is with the claims in your patent, and this is why it makes good sense to hire a competent patent attorney to ensure you get it right.

After the patent application is filed with the USPTO, a patent examiner is assigned to the case, and over the course of the next 6-24 months he or she will conduct a thorough search of the prior art to verify that your idea is novel. The results of this search will be reported back to the attorney who filed the patent application, and a timeframe (usually about three months) will be allowed for response to the report, and possible amendments to the original claims to accommodate the prior art. Ultimately, the application will be either granted or abandoned. The entire process from beginning to end can take up to several years, so be prepared to wait.

> Because of the long delays that are now typical in successfully filing for a patent, many fast-moving product innovation companies are seeking interim and almost immediate protection over their patentable IP by filing so-called provisional patents.[25] Such an application establishes a one year period of protection for the inventor without any substantial review from the USPTO and without open disclosure of the idea. At the end of the one year provisional period, the inventor has the option of either filing a formal patent application, or withdrawing the provisional filing and hence eliminating his eligibility for future patent protection.

In the end, filing for a patent or a provisional patent is a relatively straightforward process, and one that should not intimidate or discourage you. The more difficult question might simply be: "Should you, or should you not patent your idea?" As stated previously, the key tradeoff that you must weigh into this decision is the tradeoff between the Federal protection that you are granted in a patent versus the possibility that your competition will get to see explicitly all of the details about your idea in the patent. In cases where the idea itself is complex and difficult to fully contain within a finite number of written "claims," you might conclude that filing for a patent presents a greater risk of piracy than keeping the idea secret from your competition. Indeed, in Chapter 2, you learned that Brunelleschi adopted a strategy

---

[25] See also: [http://www.uspto.gov/web/offices/pac/provapp.html]

of patenting some of his ideas, while choosing to keep other ideas secret using such methods as encoded notebook records.

Trade secrets

To address the need to protect elements of intellectual property that, for whatever reasons, you judge to be best protected as secrets from your competition, the Federal government also recognizes such things as *trade secrets*. Unlike patents, which are open disclosures of information, a trade secret is intentionally kept secret, as the name implies. Many bits of intellectual property may be captured and protected as trade secrets including: a formula for a chemical compound, an apparatus for manufacturing a product, a manufacturing process, computer software, or valuable business information like marketing information or a list of customers.

> In general, a trade secret "may consist of commercial or technical information that is used in a business and offers an advantage over competitors who do not know or use such information."[26]

Legal aspects of trade secrets. The Uniform Trade Secrets Act of 1985[27] established a *trade secret* to be "the whole or any portion or phase of any scientific or technical information, design, process, procedure, formula, improvement, confidential business or financial information, listing of names, addresses, or telephone numbers, or other information relating to any business or profession which is secret and of value." This key piece of Federal legislation further establishes that "to be a trade secret the owner thereof must have taken measures to prevent the secret from becoming available to persons other than those selected by the owner to have access thereto for limited purposes."

---

[26] "The Theft of Trade Secrets is a Federal Crime," by Silverman, A. B., *Journal of Materials, (JOM)*, 49 (11) (1997), pp. 63.

[27] http://nsi.org/Library/Espionage/usta.htm

A key requirement on behalf of the owner, in order to maintain ownership over something that he or she considers to be a trade secret, is that they "must have taken measures to prevent the secret from becoming available." In layman's terms, it means that you can keep anything secret that you like, but to get Federal protection against the piracy of that secret you have to demonstrate that you worked pretty hard to prevent it from becoming known. This issue of the responsibility to maintain the secret will be discussed further when I talk about intellectual property strategies.

Although the Uniform Trade Secrets Act of 1985 established Federal guidelines for the protection of trade secrets, it wasn't until the passage of the U.S. Economic Espionage Act of 1996 (which became effective on January 1, 1997) that Federal government took a firm position of protecting the rights of ownership for trade secrets, in the same manner as trademarks or patents. As trade secrets have become as common, or even more common than patents as a vehicle to protect intellectual property, this 1996 legislation and the Federal protection that it ensures, is quite significant for any modern day inventors.

Strategic aspects of trade secrets. A classic example of a trade secret that has brought substantial wealth to its owner is the formula for Coca-Cola®. Over 125 years ago and long before the Federal government officially recognized and protected trade secrets, the Coca-Cola® Company decided that the best way to protect their existing market, and grow new markets, for the soft drink was to take great measures to prevent its formula from leaking out, while openly advertising that the secret existed.[28]

Today, the formula for Coca-Cola® and the means by which the Coca-Cola® company capitalized on this trade secret are often cited as the archetypical example of how best to use a trade secret in business. In addition to the obvious motive to keep critical technical information private, the Coca-Cola® company decided to use the trade secret as a basic element of their marketing strategy - hyping the formula as a closely held trade secret known only to a few employees, mostly executives. This approach built value in the trade secret by creating market awareness and a desire to have that particular secret formula.

---

[28] *For God, Country, and Coca-Cola: The Definitive History of the Great American Soft Drink and the Company That Makes It*, by Mark Pendergrast, Basic Books (2000)

The decision of whether to protect an element of intellectual property through patenting or trade secret, inevitably involves the consideration of your marketing strategy for the intellectual property. If you want to create hype for your idea (as the Coca-Cola® Company did very effectively) you might lean towards the "mystique" of a trade secret. On the other hand, if your goal is to sell the idea outright, you probably want to patent it so that the acquiring company knows exactly what they are buying and have clearly defined ownership rights.

Ostensibly, any novel idea can be protected by either a patent or by a trade secret. In practice however, ideas that might be easier to recreate upon observation tend to be protected through patenting, whereas ideas that are subtle and difficult to recreate upon observation tend to be protected through trade secret.

A more complete comparison of the pros and cons of patents and trade secrets is given in the accompanying table. The basic message to take away from this comparison is that patents and trade secrets each possess advantages and disadvantages, and they are somewhat complimentary by nature. Later when I discuss strategies to protect and build value in your intellectual property portfolio I will further explore the complimentary nature of these two mechanisms.

	Pros	Cons
Patents	•Clear and clean ownership •Vehicle for licensure/sale	•Open disclosure •Limited scope and duration •Cost of filing
Trade Secrets	•No disclosure •Unlimited scope and duration •No *direct* cost to secure	•Requires substantial effort to secure and maintain •Can be difficult to license/sell

Comparison of patents and trade secrets as mechanisms to protect intellectual property ownership rights.

Copyrights

The concept of the copyright originated in this country during Colonial times as a means for regulating copying rights in the publishing of books and maps. At that time, the printing industry was one of the most rapidly growing *high-tech* industries in the country. Interestingly, although Benjamin Franklin opposed the idea of patents to protect inventions, he (as the owner of a printing shop and an early innovator of printing technologies) agreed with the idea of protecting printers against the wrongful reproduction of their printed works.

> Today copyright law covers intellectual property in nearly every industry including the obvious ones of sound recordings, films, photographs, and printed publications, as well as any other industry in which critical intellectual property is reduced to printed or recorded format.

Legal aspects of copyrights. The Federal legislation that provides protection to copyright owners is the Copyright Act of 1976. Within this legislation, a *copyright* is defined as an <u>original</u> work of authorship that has a <u>modicum of creativity</u>, and is <u>fixed in a tangible medium</u> of expression. Furthermore, a copyright owner is granted the exclusive right to: 1) reproduce the work, 2) make derivative works, 3) distribute copies of the work, and 4) perform or display the work in public.

By Federal law, copyright-ownership protection begins automatically as soon as you "affix the original work in any tangible medium of expression" (e.g., transfer it from your mind to a piece of paper). In other words, you don't have to register your copyright with the Federal government you only have to fix your name to the work as the originating author for Federal protection to be granted. That said, registration of a copyright with the U.S. Copyright Office allows you to obtain enhanced damages in the event of a lawsuit, and oftentimes is a practical necessity in order for you to establish clear ownership.

Like patents, copyrights have a limited term of ownership. For individuals, the period of Federal copyright protection is the lifetime of the author plus 70 years. For works made for hire, and copyrights owned by businesses and other institutions, the period of Federal copyright protection is 90 years from first publication or 120 years from creation.

Strategic aspects of copyrights. The main reason for overhaul of U.S. copyright law through the passage of the 1976 Copyright Act, was the dramatic growth in the use of the copyrights as a means of protecting intellectual property in emerging high-tech industries like the software industry.

> All product innovation businesses use, whether consciously or unconsciously, copyright protection to cover certain aspects of their intellectual property. Examples include instructional manuals, technical publications, marketing brochures, etc.

Indeed, once an "original work of authorship" is created and distributed, the only means that exists for the author or organization to retain ownership is through copyright. Any inventor or small-business entrepreneur should automatically consider all written or recorded work they produce to be copyright-able, and they should be diligent and explicit in establishing their ownership of that copyright – especially for pieces of work that are critical to the business enterprise. Which pieces of work are critical to the business enterprise? Well, that question will have different answers depending on the type of product being marketed, and the overall IP-protection and marketing strategy that is being used to build value in the technology, but I will discuss several cases in the last subsection of this chapter.

Trademarks

A *trademark* is defined as a word, group of words, or symbol, which serves to identify the source of the product and distinguish the product from products made by a different source. A trademark is identified by the symbols ™ (not yet registered) and ® (registered). Going back to a previous example, the Coca-Cola® company has trademarked the name "Coca-Cola®," as well as the stylized logo version of the name:[29]

Coca-Cola® trademarked logo

Legal aspects of trademarks. In the late 1700's, Thomas Jefferson also proposed that certain symbols that were of value to commerce (e.g., the marks of sailcloth makers) should be protected under Federal law. Unlike support of Federal legislation for patent protection, trademark protection failed to gain Congressional support until the late 1800's. In 1946, Congress passed the Lanham Act (15 U.S.C. § 1051–1127), which currently defines federal protection and registration for trademarks, and is administered by the USPTO. In many states, state laws provide additional protections to those afforded by the Federal laws.

Under the Lanham Act, trademark rights are developed through use of the trademark. As a mark is used, consumers begin to associate the mark with a particular product. Through this association, the mark becomes a symbol of the company's reputation. Once trademark rights are developed through use, a company can apply for Federal trademark registration to enhance trademark rights. The lifetime of a trademark is the length of time that it is used by the business in the course of commerce. So once a business goes out of business its trademarks are free for reproduction or use by other parties. As an example, the former owners of Pan Am or TWA airlines could not sue you if you decided to use their formerly trademark-protected symbols for your own purposes!

Strategic aspects of trademarks. The main reason that companies create and maintain trademarks is in order to facilitate the marketing of their products or services. A trademark is meant to symbolize the

---

[29] The name "Coca-Cola®" and the "Coca-Cola®" logo are registered copyrights owned by Coca-Cola® Company in the U.S. and other countries, and are re-produced here for the sole purpose of providing a positive example of how trademarks can be used effectively in identifying and marketing a portfolio of intellectual property.

goodwill and reputation of a company to its customers. So consistent with the Federal law, the value of a trademark is determined by its effectiveness in establishing product identity and attracting customers to use the product in preference to the competition. When a customer sees, for example, the "Coca-Cola®" trademark on a soft drink product, the customer automatically knows the pedigree and quality of the product from prior experience with the product. Hence, the trademark implies a level of quality and experience in the product upon which the customer can rely.

> The strategic value in developing and using trademarks is that, if done correctly, the trademark becomes a shorthand form of advertising – a means to communicate key attributes about the product to the potential users without having to expose significant details that might better be kept secret.

Again, the Coca-Cola® company seized this very opportunity by promoting their trade-secret formula as the key ingredient that made their product superior. At the same time, they identified that formula with the trademark-protected name: Coca-Cola® and the trademark-protected symbol reproduced previously. Over time, this marketing strategy led to a general acceptance on the part of the soft-drink-buying public that "Coca-Cola®" was synonymous with good-quality soft drinks!

Building market value in your intellectual property portfolio

At this point in the discussion, you should have a much better understanding for the four main types of intellectual property that you might deal with as an inventor and entrepreneur: patents, trade secrets, copyrights, and trademarks. In this final section of the chapter, I will discuss how these four types of IP can be used selectively, and in a complimentary fashion, in order to best-protect your ideas from piracy, while also allowing you to build the greatest market value in your ideas.

Be careful not to be overprotective. Your goal is not to prevent your IP from getting out altogether. Rather, your goal is to protect key elements of the IP from piracy while you build notoriety for, and value in, your IP portfolio.

In the past few sections of this chapter I have referred to Coca-Cola® as a convenient (and commonly known) example to illustrate how trademarks and trade secrets can be coupled together in an overall marketing strategy and in an effort to build value in a given product or technology. At this point I would like to begin the discussion of building market value in your intellectual property portfolio by discussing two more recent examples from the computer industry – one that illustrates a successful intellectual property and marketing strategy, and one that illustrates a not-so-successful strategy.

An example of what to do (Intel®). The market for microelectronics has literally exploded within the short period of my career (i.e., roughly 25 years). At the time I began work as an engineer in the early 1980's, Apple Computers, Inc. IBM, Inc., and Microsoft® were locked in the epic battle discussed in Chapter 3 to define an entirely new computing platform – the desktop computer. As each decade has passed since, the number of computing devices has grown exponentially, and the total revenues created by these products in the market has grown exponentially as well.

At the heart of these computing systems are tiny *microelectronic* components that provide the "brainpower" to the devices. While Apple Computers and IBM were working hard to dominate the desktop computer market, another company was quietly growing to mega-giant status as a component provider to these giant corporations – the Intel® Corporation. Intel's product line includes some of the most commonly used microprocessors on the planet, and its market domination has been established through a combination of savvy intellectual property development and protection, and savvy marketing.

How did Intel® become so market dominant? Certainly, the technologies that are embedded within their high-performance product line are partially responsible for the success of the company. However, technology alone does not guarantee market success. As most people recognize, the market for high-tech computing devices is driven mainly by price. Indeed, the dramatic growth in this market over the past few decades is a testimony to the industry's ability to deliver a dizzying array of product offerings at "Wal-Mart" prices!

Who doesn't own a cell phone or a personal computer, or an X-Box®, or an iPod®, or . . . ? We have all become insatiable users of high-performance, low-cost electronic devices. Of course, this presents a great market opportunity for the device manufacturers, but what about their suppliers, like Intel®? If the pricing competition is tough for the device manufacturers, like IBM and Apple, then the competition for market-dominance must be lethal for those who supply the stuff inside the devices.

Which brings us to the point of appreciating the brilliance of Intel' intellectual-property protection and marketing strategy. Have you ever heard the phrase *Intel Inside®*?

That's right. This simple trademarked phrase is one of the main reasons that the Intel® Corporation has been able to separate themselves from a whole host of un-recognizable competitors in the market to provide invisible "stuff" to the microelectronics-device industry.[30] This trademarked phrase represents a visible and identifiable connection between customer and product, and in this case a product with which the customer has no direct contact! This simple phrase is the recognizable "wrapper" that Intel® has used to encapsulate its extensive intellectual

---

[30] The phrase "Intel Inside®," the "Intel Inside®" logo, and the name "Intel®" are copyrights owned by Intel® Corporation in the U.S. and other countries, and are reproduced here for the sole purpose of providing a positive example of how trademarks can be used effectively in identifying and marketing a portfolio of intellectual property.

property portfolio – a vast array of patented devices, trade secret know-how, and copyright-protected software and firmware.

The genius of this simple phrase is in the fact that the Intel® Corporation recognized that the value of their extensive intellectual property portfolio was tied directly to sales in a market where sales were mainly driven by price. In this market, Intel® recognized that just having a better product wasn't enough. So the marketing strategy was established, and the trademarked catch phrase of "Intel Inside®" was born. The result today is that few personal computers leave the factory without "Intel Inside®." If one day the Intel® Corporation decided to divest themselves of this intellectual property portfolio, you can be sure that the simple phrase "Intel Inside®" would be part of the portfolio up for sale!

> In order to create a bias in the market that would allow their products to be sold at a premium price, Intel® recognized that they had to increase customer awareness for the superiority of the product line, and hence develop increased market demand that would encourage device manufacturers to include Intel® products.

An example of what not to do (Craigslist®). Let me further illustrate the process of building market value in your intellectual property portfolio by explaining an example of how not to do it. This example also comes from the computer industry, but now we are talking about software and service companies in that industry, rather than device manufacturers. The example I would like to discuss is that of Craigslist® – the new age answer to old-school classified ads.

If you happen to be one of the few people left in the country who hasn't yet used Craigslist®, let me briefly describe the company and the software and services it provides. Craigslist® was founded in the San Francisco Bay area in the late 1990's, around the time that the "dot-com" industry was starting to bust. Apparently, the company was founded as a public service, of sorts, for professionals in that industry and with the specific goal of providing a low-cost, online resource for job postings.

Today, Craigslist® hosts an estimated 300 million ads and over 1 billion website "hits" per year covering all types of products and services and extending throughout all major geographic markets in the country. Craigslist®'s revenues are estimated to total around $80M-$100M annually, which sounds great – right? Well, you might compare this number with an industry estimate of approximately $1B for an equivalent number of lost classified listings in the newspaper industry!

The impact that Craigslist® has had on our society is being felt most heavily by the newspaper industry, whose revenues are derived largely from classified and commercial ads (rather than the modest newsstand price). Indeed, most major newspapers in this country are experiencing very difficult financial times, and many newspapers are going out of business due to their inability to cope with the changing classified-ad market.

Now, I am not criticizing Craigslist® for putting newspapers out of business. To the contrary, I am applauding Craigslist® for striking upon a new idea (Web-based classified ads), and promoting the idea to a degree that it has become the mainstream norm. Indeed, the very name "Craigslist" has become synonymous with Web-based classified advertising, and few people across the country haven't used, or at least heard about, the service. My reason for describing Craiglist® as an example of what NOT to do is that it is a very visible and well-known company that just happens to be realizing only a small fraction of the potential value of its intellectual property portfolio.

Whether by design (e.g., the benevolent good nature of the company officers) or by accident, the truth about Craigslist® is that, in business circles, it is seen as a huge missed opportunity. The fact that Craigslist® is causing billion-dollar annual losses in the printed newspaper industry demonstrates that the potential value of the Craigslist® product and service portfolio is factors of ten higher than their annual revenues.

Few new technology or product offerings grow to billion-dollar potential, and have the capacity to revolutionize or destroy mainstream markets like the printed newspaper industry. Indeed, Craigslist® is seen as a technology portfolio that could have had that potential. However, by establishing a new product and providing it as a free resource to most users (Craigslist® only charges fees for a small fraction of its ads – mainly job ads in a few of the larger metropolitan markets like San Francisco, Los Angeles, New York, Chicago, etc.), Craigslist® has essentially eliminated corporate competition, but also eliminated the potential for them to realize any substantial revenues from their own products.

Could it have been done differently? Possibly. Imagine if the founders of Craigslist® had seen the potential for their collection of software products and services to become market dominant, and ultimately to have billion-dollar impact to the printed newspaper industry. If so they might have taken great care to create an intellectual property portfolio that could not easily have been reproduced by competition, then they would have launched a strategic marketing campaign aimed at raising awareness of the product and growing market share, WITHOUT having to give the product away. The end result could have been a corporate acquisition of Craigslist® by one of the leading newspaper companies (LA Times, Chicago Tribune) for a billion-dollar price tag, and in an effort to create a whole new revenue stream for the newspaper, and a national footprint for classified ads!

Do you remember the billion-dollar merger of America Online (AOL) and Times-Warner in 2000? The same "pot of gold" could have been at the end of the Craigslist® "rainbow," but the apparent marketing and intellectual property protection strategies (or lack thereof) seem to have made that possibility remote.

Connecting your IP-protection and IP-marketing strategies. If you now understand that building value in your intellectual property is the key to your ultimate success in the product innovation business world, then you can easily see why thoughtful and deliberate marketing of your intellectual property is a critically important step towards success. The need to connect your strategies for IP protection and marketing should seem obvious at this point in the discussion, but I am amazed at how many inventors and small-business entrepreneurs fail to connect the two things together. Indeed, it seems far too commonplace in product innovation business for the roles of IP strategy and protection to be compartmentalized and separated from the roles of business development and marketing.

Often in product innovation businesses there exist separate executive-level positions like Chief Technology Officer (CTO) and Vice President for Business Development. Rightfully so these positions are typically filled by people with expertise in the areas of IP strategy and marketing strategy, respectively, and the officers who fill these positions are held responsible for *tactical* execution in those areas. The issue that often occurs though, is that the company fails to establish a strategic vision that overlays on top of, and connects together, these two critically linked areas of executive responsibility. In essence, the *right hand* – the VP for Marketing – is left not knowing what the *left hand* – the CTO – is doing. So the public image that the VP of Marketing is creating doesn't necessarily line up with, or more critically *build value in,* the intellectual property portfolio that the CTO is amassing.

This is an obvious problem to "sniff out" in small companies. Just ask the VP of Marketing if he understands the structure of the IP portfolio, or ask the CTO if she agrees with the current marketing strategy. If you get frustrated looks, then you know that the CEO hasn't done his job of connecting these two critical functions!

So what can be done to remedy this situation? Well, with all humility speaking as a former CTO of a small company, I would assert that the starting point for constructing a solid, top-level strategy for coupling IP-protection and marketing efforts is a thorough and thoughtful assessment of the market opportunities. At the end of the day, it is a business, and business thrives where there are market opportunities. If you leave it up to the technologist (e.g., the CTO) or the patent attorney to define the IP-protection strategy, they will likely conclude that every good idea they have invented should be patented or protected as a trade secret.

A good VP of Marketing should understand the market opportunities, and with a reasonably complete understanding of the capabilities encompassed by the intellectual property within the company, this same person should be able to write a prescription for how best to package the intellectual property in the form of products or for licensure/sale to another business entity. In short, a truthful assessment of the market opportunities should lead the executive management team towards the development of a strategy that defines which elements of intellectual property have the greatest potential value and how best to protect this property while increasing its value through active marketing efforts.

Going back to the market-assessment discussions in Chapter 3, you might recall that a key issue for you to understand early in the development of your enterprise is the *need* in the customer base for your invention. Indeed, if you did a good job in your early market research, you now have a very clear idea of the attributes of your invention that the customer needs. Furthermore, you have a sense of the price that the customer will pay, and some thoughts as to the cost that you will have to pay in producing that product. These elements of market analysis provide the connection between your marketing strategy and your IP-protection strategy.

> The attributes in your invention that you see as being most valuable to the market are the intellectual property attributes that are most critical for you to protect.

At the outset, you might have seen your invention as a single, patentable idea. After you have absorbed yourself in the feedback that you have gotten from prospective customers, you should be better positioned to define the attributes that are most valuable, and to consider the appropriate intellectual-property mechanism(s) through which to protect them. In some situations, a single patent of the idea is still the best means of protection. However, in other situations, a combination of patents and trade secrets might give you a stronger position. Unfortunately, there is no right answer to this question. The best path depends on the particular market and your overall business goals (e.g., do I want to manufacture these products forever, or do I want to sell this business to someone else some day). To account for these uncertainties, I usually recommend that my clients consider diversifying their intellectual property portfolio using several protection mechanisms.

Diversifying and balancing the IP portfolio to allow for uncertainties. Until now, I have referred several times to intellectual property *portfolios* without ever taking the time to define what I mean by the word *portfolio*. At a very basic level, I use the word *portfolio* to mean a collection of intellectual property – potentially of all types (i.e., patents, trade secrets, copyrights, and trademarks). Practically, I want the word *portfolio* to imply a thoughtfully constructed collection of intellectual property that is inter-connected in some way, or that is *collectively* being marketed under a single marketing effort.

Let me expand on this second definition of *intellectual property portfolio* using the accompanying graphical depiction of a three-legged table. In the most-general case, an intellectual property portfolio can include technologies that are protected through patents, trade secret, and copyright laws (three legs of the table). If properly assembled and coupled to an over-riding marketing strategy, a distinct trademark or group of trademarks, which is depicted as the top of the table, easily identifies this portfolio. The *tabletop* – collection of trademarks – is the most conspicuous and easily recognizable element of the portfolio, while the *legs* – the collection of patents, trade secrets, and copyrights – provide the *substance* to the portfolio.

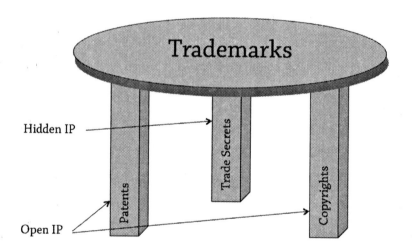

Balancing the Intellectual Property Portfolio.

In many instances, intellectual property portfolios are simpler in structure than the three-legged table depicted in the figure. In the case of Coca-Cola®, the portfolio consists of a few trademarks and a trade secret formula (this might be an over-simplification of the Coca-Cola® Company's portfolio, but I'll use a little artistic license here to make a point!). In other instances, intellectual property portfolios can be quite complex – including all elements of IP (patents, trade secrets, and copyrights) and multiple pieces of each element. This is likely the case for the Intel® Corporation and their family of Pentium® microprocessors. More importantly, in most cases of businesses that penetrate into multiple markets, and/or whose product line lives through numerous revision cycles, an IP-protection strategy that works well in one situation might not work best in another situation.

As an example, prior to the early 1990's Bill Gates had a very simple IP-protection strategy for the Microsoft® Corporation – all pieces of software were copyright protected, and all know-how was protected through trade secret practices. By the early 1990's, he came to realize that many features and functionalities in his suite of products were being mimicked in a litany of third-party software products, many of which were being offered as *free-ware* – software that is given away instead of sold. Indeed, Mr. Gates came to see that his company's pay-for-product revenue model was at risk due to the growing use of Web-based advertising revenue streams coupled with free-ware products.

So in response to this threat, Microsoft® did an about-face on the topic of patenting of its intellectual property. Between 1995 and 2005, the company secured approximately 5,000 patents on essentially every feature and functionality that it was incorporating into new-generation products (that's about 2 patents awarded each and every business day for 10 years!) Backing this move up, Microsoft® also started aggressively suing third-party software companies for infringement, and almost singlehandedly, started turning the tide in the marketplace away from free-ware products!

A single IP-protection strategy might not serve to best protect your interests in multiple markets or in a single market that evolves over time. In response to this issue, one should consider building some level of balance and diversity in their IP portfolio from the outset by using all IP-protection mechanisms. In some businesses, you can be very successful using a single IP-protection mechanism (e.g., patents). But in most situations balance and diversity among the different types of IP can better position you for multiple market-entry strategies, and better protect you against unforeseen changes in the market.

Constructing your IP portfolio. What then is the best structure for your intellectual property portfolio? Should you patent a particular invention or keep it as a trade secret? Does your idea have multiple elements to it, each one of which that might prefer a different protection strategy? Most importantly, what are the intrinsic attributes of the portfolio that you are trying to market, and what is the image that you are trying to create through effective trademark identification?

These questions are exactly the questions you should be asking yourself at this point in time. If the questions all make sense, then I have accomplished the main objective of this chapter – to educate you on the critical importance of intellectual property to your enterprise, and to get you started in creating your own intellectual property protection and marketing strategy. Unfortunately, I can't possibly answer all of these questions, because the answers are very dependent on your specific ideas and the market(s) into which you are trying to launch new products. The answers also depend a great deal on your ultimate business goals. So rather than writing you a "prescription" for your own IP-protection strategy, I will give you several very practical ideas about how to construct a strategy that best fits your needs.

> First, if you wish to build up a company and then sell it to the highest bidder within a few years, or you wish to sell your IP portfolio outright and avoid building up a company, it is likely that you will realize the greatest value out of patented IP.

Companies who are in the business of acquiring smaller companies or IP portfolios tend to look down upon trade secrets simply because it is difficult to prove, absolutely, that the secret hasn't leaked out. So in order to be a good target for acquisition, you need to make sure that at least key elements of your IP are patented.

> Second, if you are planning to build a company and keep it indefinitely, the best place to look for an IP-protection strategy might be within the very market that you are trying to penetrate.

Find out what other companies in the market consider to be their intellectual property, and explore how they have decided to protect that property. Also look for corporate acquisitions and/or technology offerings within that market and learn how technology portfolios were bundled and marketed for sale. Basically, educate yourself on the business of intellectual property management and sale within your specific market of interest.

> Third, regardless of your business goals (i.e., to sell your IP outright, or to build a business and sell products) build value in your unique intellectual property through a thoughtful combination of trademarks and a marketing strategy that promotes the trademarked IP.

Utilize this combined IP-protection and marketing strategy to build value in your IP portfolio. As described earlier, a truthful assessment of the market opportunities should lead the executive management team towards the development of a strategy that defines which elements of intellectual property have the greatest potential market value and how best to increase this value through active marketing efforts.

> Fourth, regardless of how you decide to divide your critical IP between patents and trade secrets, establish a plan for copyright-protecting all valuable written and recorded documents.

Summary

In Chapter 2 you learned how the son of a 14th-century trade worker dedicated his life to rising out of the lower socio-economic class he had inherited from his father. He did so through a lot of creativity and personal drive, but the single issue that enabled his ascendancy into the aristocracy of the Renaissance was the recognition that he could make money off of his unique ideas, *if he was thoughtful and careful in how he protected them against loss while he promoted them for profit.*

Four hundred years later, Thomas Jefferson became the founding father of intellectual property law in the U.S. by similarly recognizing how important the ownership of novel ideas could be to creating new business and commerce within this country. Although he failed to see the impact of his vision within his own lifetime, the lasting tribute to this great 18th-century American aristocrat is that the laws that he helped establish have provided the pathway for millions of Americans – including countless tradesmen and workers in America's lower socio-economic classes – to capitalize on their ideas and rise to a higher economic class.

Today, all inventors and entrepreneurs start on an equal Constitutional footing that has come to almost parallel the inalienable rights of life, liberty, and the pursuit of happiness. If you have a good idea and live in this country, ipso facto, your Federal government will protect your rights to use that idea for profit and personal gain. The only things you have to do are: 1) prove to the Government that it's your idea, and 2) prove to the marketplace that it's a good idea.

Through the last two chapters, you should have gained insight into how to assess the market opportunity for your idea and how to build value in it through a combination of protection and marketing of your unique intellectual property. Now, let's talk about the next critical piece of *The Inventor's Puzzle* – how you turn your idea into a marketable product!

5

Evolving the Design: An Introduction to Product Engineering

"A good scientist is a person with original ideas. A good engineer is a person who makes a design that works with as few original ideas as possible."

– Freeman Dyson

In the good old days (roughly 30-40 years ago), a "designer" was an engineer who was responsible for developing a detailed design for something including making drawings or models that demonstrated the key features of the design. Thanks to the explosion of the fashion industry in the past several decades, the common definition of the term "designer" has completely changed and is now more popularly associated with artists than it is with engineers.

For example, if you were to buy a designer chair, you would expect that it would have a very stylish look, and possibly the embroidered name of a famous French artist sewn into its back. You probably wouldn't expect that the chair was built using very cleverly contrived mech-anical components or to be intentionally contoured to best fit your body. So, speaking as an engineer and not a

designer, if the chair ends up being the most uncomfortable and least-used chair in your house – don't complain to me, you decided to buy a *designer chair* not a *well-designed chair!*

Kidding aside, the terms designer and well designed are neither synonymous nor mutually exclusive. Indeed, a designer product might be a well-designed product and vice versa. The reason that I am toying with the meanings of these phrases is to bring up a key attribute for any successful new product – the positive impression that it leaves with the customer. As an engineer, I tend to place a higher premium on functional requirements such as quality and performance. However as a businessman, I have learned to respect deeply the marketing genius that can create good business out of frilly and stylish features. Indeed, I can think of many modestly innovative products that achieved dramatic success in the market through proper packaging and image creation.

> Most successful products are designed to create a particular impression as much as they are designed to serve a particular function.

For example, do you or someone you know own a pair of Crocs®? Of course you do. Who doesn't? I don't think that very many engineers could have possibly predicted that brightly colored plastic clogs would become designer footwear! However, George B. Boedecker, Jr., the founder of Crocs®, certainly saw the potential market appeal. And fortunately for his company, a modestly innovative idea was coupled with a very innovative marketing strategy to produce a market revolution.

Which was more important in this business success story? Mr. Boedecker's brilliant idea of using a lightweight foam plastic material to create a new type of shoe, *or* the hard work performed by his technical staff to convert that designer idea into a well-designed product? As an engineer and businessman, I can say with certainty that both the designer idea and the well-designed product were critical to the success of Crocs®. Indeed, and as discussed extensively in Chapters 3 and 4, any successful product innovation business starts with a good idea that has market appeal. However:

> A good idea with market appeal will never make it into a viable product without a disciplined engineering-development process that roots out the Achilles heels of the design – the weak points that, if left alone, would diminish or eliminate the market appeal.

Before jumping into our discussion of product-development engineering, I just have to point out that the early design for Crocs® included no strap across the Achilles tendon, as is common in other clog-style shoes. After early market studies, the company decided to add the strap in order to improve utility for a wider array of uses. So . . . [drum roll please] . . . one could say that the lack of the *Achilles-tendon strap* was an *Achilles heel* of the original design! (Okay, maybe engineers don't tell the best marketing jokes!)

The effect of product image on product requirements

The starting point for this product-development discussion is the *product image* – the impression that you want to create in the customers' eyes through your trademark labeling and product-marketing strategy.[31] In one extreme, you might determine that your best opportunity for success in the market is to build the best-quality product that you can regardless of cost, and to highlight quality in your trademark and marketing campaign. In another extreme, you might determine that your best opportunity for success is to create a *designer mystique* in the minds of the customer base by offering them a product that is more recognizable for its stylish design. Or possibly, you might determine that your best approach is somewhere between these extremes: a good-quality product that is attractive in its style and form and a marketing campaign and trademark strategy that promotes both qualities.

Early in this book I discussed *right-brain* – creative – thought processes and *left-brain* – structured and organized – thought processes. I bring this concept back up because we have just reached a point in solving *The*

---

[31] *Marketing Aesthetics: The Strategic Management of Brands, Identity and Image,* by Bernd H. Schmitt and Alex Simonson, The Free Press, a Division of Simon and Schuster, Inc. (1997)

Inventor's Puzzle where both halves of the brain must work together! Understanding the customer base and the market for your product is mainly an exercise in gathering and organizing data (i.e., left-brain). Whereas interpreting that information in the interest of evolving your product and defining the image that you want the product to create in the customer's mind is mainly an exercise in creative thought (i.e., right-brain). Finally, integrating these factors together to compile a complete set of product-development requirements and develop a structured product-development plan is back to exercising the left half of the brain and taxing your organizational skills.

If you are like most engineers, then you probably are comfortable with the data-gathering and program-planning exercises that constitute the beginning and end points of this activity. If you are like most artists and many inventors then you are most comfortable with the creative activity in the middle devoted to defining the product image and marketing strategy. Assuming that you are not comfortable in both rolls, as is the case with most people, now is the time when you need to connect with someone who compliments your talents and with whom you can work together to hammer out both the creative and structured aspects of this planning exercise.

Answering this question of product image is difficult and may be one of the biggest challenges in creating a marketable product from your invention. Of course, the best strategy is very dependent on the type of product you are developing and the market you are targeting. Some markets care little about image and value only quality and performance. Other markets (like the market for designer clothes) are more driven by image than any other single attribute. Ultimately, you, your marketing expert, and possibly your business partners who share a vested interest in the success of the product, must come to some agreement as to the image that you want to promote in the product.

The decision on product image and actions that you take to create that image (such as through the selection of trademarks), can solidify your intellectual property strategy and will contribute significantly to the set of requirements that will drive the product-development process forward.

Developing a complete set of product-development requirements

In Chapter 3, I said that any successful design must be rooted in a clear set of requirements that are derived from an analysis of the market and represent a "mathematical" definition of the customer base – a measurable set of metrics that should ensure that *when you build it, they will buy it*! Given the preceding discussion of product image, it should now be clear that the requirements must encompass both the physical metrics that satisfy the customers' needs (e.g., cost, size, performance, function, etc.) and the less tangible elements that leave the customer with the desired impression (e.g., style, image, convenience, etc.).

This sounds like a pretty complete set of requirements, doesn't it? Well, believe it or not, this set of so-called *product requirements* is only a subset of the complete set of requirements that is necessary to drive the product-development activity forward! What then constitutes a complete set of product-development requirements? In general, a complete set of requirements will include the following four subsets of requirements:[32]

Complete Set of Product-Development Requirements

Product Requirements describe the product from the perspective of the customer including physical metrics and desired product image.

Business Requirements describe the product from the perspective of the business and capture what the product must accomplish for the business and its investors to be successful.

Process Requirements describe the standardized processes and practices that the product-development team must follow in executing the product-development program.

Regulatory Requirements describe design-certification requirements for products that are subject to government regulatory control.

---

[32] *Effective Requirements Practices*, by Ralph R. Young, Addison-Wesley Publishers (2001)

I have already addressed the *product requirements*, and will now describe the remaining three subsets of requirements that drive product design.

Business requirements. Just as the *product requirements* describe what the customer wants, the *business requirements* describe what you (the businessperson) and/or your business partners need in the product design in order for it to contribute to your business enterprise. Among these business requirements might be requirements that reflect the business's intellectual property protection and marketing strategy (e.g., use of trademarks, brands, and inclusion of patent-protected IP). Additionally, it is very common to establish business requirements related to the manufacturing, distribution, and sales of the product like: a) the use of specific strategic partners, b) restriction to certain geographic regions or countries, and c) definition of acceptable *profit margins* – the difference between the manufacturing, distribution, and sales cost and the market price of the product.

> The *business requirements* will be the most hotly debated requirements by your investors, business partners, and Board of Directors or Advisors. These requirements will also be the most-closely tracked by these people as they represent the linkage between the product design and business success.

Process requirements. *Process requirements* represent practical constraints imposed on the product-development team and that reflect some degree of strategic guidance or control asserted by the company over the product-development activity. For example, a maximum development cost may be imposed based on corporate financial resources. Also as will be discussed in a later section of this chapter, it is very normal for a company to require the product-development team to follow a particular development review/inspection process (e.g., Stage-Gate® Process[33]). Similarly, and in order to ensure a degree of consistency and accuracy in the product-development program, it is common for companies to require that all design information and product-testing programs are documented according to some pre-

---

[33] *Lean, Rapid, and Profitable New Product Development*, by Robert. G. Cooper and Scott J. Edgett, Published by Product Development Institute (2005)

existing quality-control standard (e.g., ISO 9000[34]). Finally, in markets where product-liability issues can be significant, process requirements will be established to ensure that all potential liability issues are addressed during the product-development program.

> The *process requirements* reflect the standardized practices of the industry into which the product is to be marketed, the company developing the product, and partnering organizations that might be working with the company.

To illustrate with an extreme example, it is often said that within the aerospace industry no new aircraft or spacecraft ever gets off the ground until the total weight of the paperwork (largely to demonstrate compliance with process requirements) exceeds the weight of the vehicle! Fortunately most markets, with the possible exception of medical technology, do not present the staggering volume of process requirements that are typical of the aerospace market!

Regulatory requirements.   For products that are subject to government regulation and/or control, a set of *regulatory requirements* must be established in order to guide the design in a direction that will ensure compliance with the pertinent regulatory restrictions. For example, if your product is a medical device, it is likely that you will have to have it certified by the FDA (Food and Drug Administration), which can be a very expensive and time-consuming process. Similarly, if your product is to be used on commercial airliners, you will likely have to have it certified by either the FAA (Federal Aviation Administration) or the DOT (Department of Transportation).

> It is very common for *regulatory requirements* to completely dominate and for regulatory testing and compliance to consume a majority of the total cost of a product-development effort.

---

[34] http://www.iso.org/iso/home.htm

If you are developing a product that will require compliance with government regulations, it is absolutely critical that you assess the regulatory requirements early, and enlist the support of people who are well versed in the applicable government regulations and testing standards. The last thing you want to do is develop a product that is deemed to be illegal due to lack of compliance with government regulations!

Organizing and managing requirements

If this lengthy list of requirements seems to be overwhelming to you, don't worry – you are having a very normal reaction to your first intimate exposure to the "horror" of life as an engineer! You are also now able to see why most engineers are trained to be *left-brain-dominant* organizers! To assemble a complete set of requirements as outlined above, organize them in a way that facilitates, not stalls, the program, and finally to manage and track changes to requirements throughout the program, is quite a task.[32]

To meet this challenge, most product-development organizations employ a hierarchical approach for organizing requirements and a strategy for subdividing requirements into categories that are parsed out to different individuals who share the responsibility of tracking, updating, and demonstrating compliance with the requirements. A typical requirements hierarchy might span three or four levels starting with a top level that includes subjective (non-measurable) business requirements and filtering down through levels of increasing detail to measurable requirements that affect component designs like "Part ABC will weigh no more than 3 oz."

For very complex products, it is normal for the requirements hierarchy to be subdivided into "branches" that each deal with a component of the total system. For example, the requirements hierarchy for a new espresso maker might be divided into the following branches: 1) system design, 2) electrical components, 3) water/steam subsystem, 4) control panel, 5) design styling, 6) testing and verification requirements, and 7) documentation. Within each branch, there would be several levels of requirements starting with the more subjective at the top, and evolving to very measurable requirements at the lower levels.

A well organized product-development team will usually be led by a program manager, who has responsibility for negotiating the final requirements with the company officers, and for alerting the company officers in the event that the program fails to achieve key requirements in the design. Usually, the program manager will also have a lead engineer on the product-development team, who has responsibility for detailed organization and management of the requirements. For simple products, the functions of lead engineer and program manager might be combined and given to a single individual, but for complex products, the functions are generally left separate.

Letting requirements drive the engineering process

As discussed briefly in Chapter 3, all engineers are trained to recognize that, in order to develop a design for a particular purpose, it is necessary *a priori* to define what the device must do in precisely measurable requirements. Otherwise, it is impossible to determine, with confidence, if the device that is ultimately built actually does what you intended it to do. So rather than recoiling in horror at a lengthy set of requirements, a good engineer will see that a well-constructed and complete set of requirements actually makes his or her life simpler.

The amount of freedom that a design engineer has to explore in the *design space* – the range of possible variations in the design – is somehow inversely related to the total number of requirements or constraints that are imposed on the design. Which is to say that, the greater the number of requirements that are imposed on the design means that there are fewer possible design variations that might be considered. From a different perspective, a complete set of requirements arms a good product-development engineer with the ammunition that he or she needs to shoot down a majority of the inferior candidate design concepts or details. The ability to sort through design concepts quickly and discard the ones that won't properly meet the requirements is a key to driving the product-development program forward.

Let me take a step backwards here and compare the process of invention with the process of product-development engineering. If you are an inventor, then when you first came up with the idea for your invention there is a good likelihood that you ran out to the garage or workshop and cobbled together a crude model of the thing that you had in mind (assuming that your invention is a mechanical device and not a piece of software or something else that is intangible). You were probably motivated to create this initial model for several reasons: 1) you wanted to see if the idea actually worked, 2) you wanted to use this model as a means to work out some *wrinkle* in the idea – a detail that was difficult for you to see in your mind, and/or 3) you wanted to have something tangible as a means to share your idea with others.

Well, these are the very same reasons that a product-development engineer might build working models of the product at various stages of the product-development program. The main difference between an inventor's first prototype model and these later-stage models is in the total number of requirements that are addressed in the designs and the rigor with which the design is tested in order to determine whether it meets these requirements. In building and testing the first prototype of your invention, you wanted to establish a bare minimum degree of functionality – a *proof-of-concept*. By the end of the product-development program, the complete set of requirements must be met by the design and demonstrated through an extensive series of tests of advanced prototypes and preproduction units.

In a very real sense, you should look at the first proof-of-concept model of your invention – built out of duct tape, bailing wire, and any other odds and ends from your garage – as the first in a lineage of engineering models that will ultimately be used by the design team to flesh out the design. Furthermore, you should recognize that that first model was built to prove compliance with some small list of requirements. Even if you didn't take the time to actually write the requirements down and record the results of your tests. The remainder of the product-development program – from proof-of-concept to final product – is simply an expansion on that first build-and-test exercise with a substantial increase in the rigor and thoroughness that is applied.

> The progress of a product-development program is measured by the number of requirements that have been met in the design and how far the remaining requirements are from being met.

It is very normal at the midpoint of a product-development program for most key requirements to be met but a few of the remaining requirements to be lacking. For example, a midpoint review might reveal that the interim design meets all functional requirements (i.e., it does what it is intended to do), and it meets the weight and size requirements, but the manufacturing studies show that the product will cost 20% more to produce than the target cost. This failure to meet a key requirement could precipitate: 1) further work to adapt the design to better meet the requirement, 2) a renegotiation of the requirement, or 3) a cancellation of the project. It all depends on how critical the requirement is and how credible the product-development team is in explaining their possible solutions to resolve the issue.

Corporate processes for managing product-development cost and risk

In modern day, product innovation businesses where new ideas are turned into advanced products on a daily basis, a standardized engineering process is critical to the success of these efforts. Indeed, most companies involved in product innovation today oversee the progress of such programs at the Board of Directors' level in a process that reflects the style by which the *Opera del Duomo* oversaw Brunelleschi's work on the Dome of Santa Maria del Fiore. Such a process is designed to move the project forward incrementally until the next major milestone is successfully completed. If something critical goes wrong along the way, the oversight committee has the power to halt the project or redirect efforts until the project is back on track.

In most product innovation businesses the progress of product-development programs is typically reviewed using a standardized template of development milestones and performance metrics and the engineering-development efforts are co-managed with other coupled efforts like market research.

There is no single standard step-by-step process for managing product-development programs. However, all such processes share some essential traits in common. First, the program is divided into a finite number of steps, each of which is planned for a finite period of time and ends in a "go/no-go" decision usually made by the CEO or Board of Directors. Second, the go/no-go decision at the end of each program step is based, at least partially, on the results of specific tests and/or analyses that are established at the outset and that assess maturity of the design and its conformance to key requirements. Third, the project is funded incrementally with funding for the following step generally allocated upon successful completion of the present step.

For example, the Federal Government applies the following three-phase process in determining funding awards to small businesses through its *Small Business Innovation Research* (SBIR) program.[35] In the next chapter, I will discuss the SBIR program as a means to get government funding to support your product-development program. At this time, I simply want to point out that even the Federal Government demands some degree of cost and risk management in their program to fund small product innovation businesses. In general, you can anticipate that anyone who is willing to write a check to support your efforts will demand some degree of cost and risk management, and they will typically enforce this through a step-by-step process of go/no-go decisions that test the progress of the design against the complete set of requirements that have been established.

	Phase I	Phase II	Phase III
Time Duration	9-12 months	24 months	Variable
Funding Allocation	$100K	$750K	Variable
Success Criteria	Proof-of-concept	Product Demonstration	Market Insertion

Three-Phase Federal SBIR Program

Summary

The world-renowned physicist Freeman Dyson apparently appreciated the essence of good engineering better than most inventors do. His quote, which was recited at the beginning of this chapter, captures the theme of this chapter and the central issue that you must confront if you

---

[35] http://www.sbir.gov/

are to create a marketable product from your idea. The process of product engineering, which is necessary to reduce your invention to practical design, is *very different* than the process of research and discovery that might have lead to your invention in the first place.

Unlike the *right-brain-dominant* – mostly creative and not driven by a set structure - exercise of invention, the exercise of product development and engineering is very much a *left-brain-dominant* – very structured and methodical – exercise. Furthermore, the key driver in product-development engineering is to reduce cost and risk while meeting requirements. Whereas, the key driver in the process of invention is to create something new! So step one in this process is for you to recognize that product development requires a certain amount of discipline, experience, and training that the average inventor might very well lack.

Hence, a key to solving this piece of *The Inventor's Puzzle* is to involve the appropriate *designer* (not the French fashion type) or team of *designers* who have the proper experience to move your design forward and to satisfy your investors by managing and minimizing the cost and risk of the product-development program. Assuming that you are not trained in this process of product development, then you *must* prepare yourself to give up ownership over the design to people who are, and you must be prepared to accept evolution of the design as a necessary step towards its commercialization.

With this, I want to turn your attention to the million-dollar question and the next piece of *The Inventor's Puzzle*: "where will you get the money that you will need to pay for the product-development program?"

6

Capitalization: An Introduction to Raising Money

"Jerry - I want you to say it with meaning, brother! . . . Show me the money."

– From the movie "Jerry Maguire"

If you're old enough to remember when Steve Martin was a stand-up comic, which I am, then you might remember his classic shtick on how to make a million dollars: "First, you get a million dollars . . . Second, don't pay taxes." Although I'm not going to endorse Steve's tax advice, I will tip my hat to the first part of the message. *To make money, generally requires that you have money.*

So is this a catch-22? After all, one of the main reasons that you are likely to be so passionate about product innovation business is that you see the possibility that it may lead you to wealth. Now I am telling you that you need money to make money! How useful is that advice? You could have just bought Steve Martin's old stand-up comedy album and got the same message and a lot more laughs for less money invested!

Before you jump to that conclusion and take me up on my earlier offer of a money-back guarantee for this book, let me say that getting working capital in order to launch a product innovation business isn't as desperate of a proposition as you might think. In fact, one of the most amazing things about this country is that there are many institutions, including many offices within the Federal and State Governments, whose sole purpose is to provide money to people like you! Indeed, getting money up front to help develop good ideas and inventions into marketable products and not having to do it all from one's "bootstraps" is in fact the way that most successful people realize the American Dream.

So assuming that you have a good product concept, a well constructed product-development program plan, and a solid business opportunity for the marketing and sales of that product, the next-most important issue that you need to contend with is the issue of raising sufficient money to get your product developed and into the market. Indeed, if you don't approach the issue of raising money (i.e., capitalization) with the same level of energy and determination as you approach the other issues discussed to this point, you will find that all of your other efforts were in vain.

Having money at the moment of conception of the invention isn't essential (i.e., you don't have to be rich to be creative), but figuring out how to secure money efficiently and in a timely fashion is essential if you are to make a viable business out of an invention. I know that there are many smart people who appear to have built their business empires from their own "bootstraps," but most of these people actually had to secure infusions of cash at one or more points along the way. For example, Bill Gates is generally considered to have built Microsoft® from his own "bootstraps," but even he had to secure $50,000 when he was in his early 20's to buy the rights to the original DOS operating system.

Maximizing your odds of success in the product innovation business world essentially requires not just good ideas but also solid financial support.

The purpose of this chapter is to discuss the various sources of working capital that may be available to you, and to compare and contrast the processes that you have to undergo to get the money and the "strings" that may be attached to those sources of money. You've surely heard the old phrase: *you can't get something for nothing*, and that is certainly true of working capital that you might secure to move your project forward. That being said, giving up something (e.g., partial ownership of your idea) early on in order to get something (i.e., working capital) that allows you to mature that idea into a product that makes money is a good business proposition.

Ultimately, the goal of this chapter is to tell you enough about the different sources of money available to you that you can make a more informed decision as to which type (or types) of money you wish to secure. More importantly, the chapter will also describe how one actually secures such money! Ultimately, I hope that you will emerge from reading this chapter with a better plan to capitalize your efforts and a realistic set of expectations about what will be involved in capitalization – both the energy expended and the cost to do so. With this financial piece of *The Inventor's Puzzle* in place your odds of success will increase dramatically.

Opening the dialogue with investors – the elevator pitch revisited

Before I talk about the types of working capital, I want to reintroduce a concept that I first discussed in Chapter 3 – *the elevator pitch* – a brief summary of your invention and the business opportunity that you are creating around that invention. As mentioned in Chapter 3, the elevator pitch originated in the business world out of the simple recognition that potential investors and strategic business partners are only interested in the facts that are pertinent to defining the business opportunity, and they want those facts presented in clear, cohesive, and concise fashion. They simply don't have the time or patience to sit through a lengthy discussion on every issue and topic that you have considered since you first conceived of your invention: they want to know in short order, whether or not your business opportunity is a good business opportunity for them.

> The elevator pitch is important to the discussion of how to secure working capital because this short abstract of your business opportunity will become the most critical first step towards securing money from any source.

Since it has been a while since I discussed the elevator pitch, I want to restate here the list of questions that constitute a good outline for constructing your pitch:

The Elevator Pitch

1. What is your product?

Describe the product you plan to make out of your invention. Keep it simple and focus on the attributes that will sell the product.

2. Who is your market?

Discuss to whom you are selling the product. How large is the market, how much of the market do you expect to be able to capture, and why?

3. Who is your competition?

Discuss who they are and what they have accomplished. Identifying successful competition is an advantage in that this proves there is good business in this market. Saying you have no competition indicates you have no understanding of the market.

4. What is your competitive advantage?

Describe how your product is different and why you have an advantage over the competition. Clearly describe your intellectual property, and your strategy for protecting it.

5. What is your revenue model?

Describe all elements of your product cost, including manufacturing, marketing and sales, and overhead costs simply. Explain how you expect to make money, and how you expect to pay your investors.

6. Who are your key leaders and who is behind the company?

Tell a little about you and your team's background and achievements. If you have a strong advisory board, tell who they are and what they have accomplished in past businesses. Describe any other investments you have already secured.

When I first discussed the elevator pitch you didn't have enough information to complete one. Hopefully by now you understand better how to gather information necessary to answer the first four questions.

In the present chapter, I will discuss financial issues that will help you construct an answer for question 5, and in the next chapter you will gain a better sense of how to answer question 6. However, don't think that you have to know everything with absolute clarity in order to construct an elevator pitch.

> Your elevator pitch will be a living thing, and it will evolve as your understanding of the opportunity evolves. Be disciplined enough to write one down, but be flexible enough to let it change as you get smarter about the enterprise.

Now, let's start our discussion of capitalization by exploring the different types of working capital that you might secure to help fund your young enterprise. For simplicity's sake I want to divide the sources of money into three categories: Government money, private-investment money, and personal money. Alternatively, if you are a fan of Clint Eastwood and his "spaghetti" westerns from the 1960's you might be amused to consider these sources of money: "good money," "bad money," and "ugly money," respectively.

good money   *bad money*   *ugly money*

Personal money – "ugly money"

In the small business world, personal money is oftentimes referred to as "4-F" money as it is generally money from Friends, Family, Founders, and Fools! This is money that you might get from your own savings account, home-equity line of credit, or from those people who are closest to you in life. It is probably the easiest money you can get because the investors usually won't scrutinize your elevator pitch and only need to have a vague notion of your business opportunity. These people believe in you and want to invest in you!

> Why do I call personal money "ugly money?" Well, if your business enterprise happens to fail the friends and family members who gave you this money will get very ugly shortly thereafter!

This might sound very comical, but it is very true. Personal money is very attractive because it might be the easiest money to get assuming you or someone you know of has a healthy bank account. However, the risk of loss of this type of money is also greatest because it is usually brought in at the earliest stage of a new enterprise (i.e., the riskiest stage). Furthermore, personal investors usually don't contribute strategic insight and guidance to the enterprise unlike professional investors who might invest at a later-stage and usually contribute guidance along with money to increase the likelihood that the enterprise will succeed.

A common trap associated with personal money is that many inventors and young entrepreneurs *want* to get money from friends and family because they sincerely want those people who are closest to them to share in the success of the enterprise. This seems like a wonderful motive to the optimistic inventor or entrepreneur, and she should feel encouraged to let these loved ones share in the up side of her efforts. However, it is critically important that she *and they* truly understand and assess the risks associated with early-stage funding of a new product innovation enterprise. Otherwise, a gesture that was meant to make her personal relationships prosper could cause them to crumble.

All professional investors understand that any particular investment opportunity comes with some likelihood of failure and financial loss. New business enterprises fail every day in the business world, and all smart investors understand that possibility and plan for it by diversifying or spreading their investments across several such ventures. In a later subsection, I will discuss the world of private-investment money, and you will come to better understand how private investors manage risk in their investments and how they work very proactively to minimize their risk of loss while maximizing the chances of success for businesses they are investing in.

At this point in the discussion and in the context of considering the use of personal investment money, you only need to ask yourself and your potential investor(s): if they knew that your business efforts might really fail (recall from Chapter 1 that one out of three new businesses that are started each year eventually fail)[7], would they still want to invest in your business? Bear in mind that most people who would invest personal money in your young business enterprise are very naïve about the risks involved in the investment. These investors are mainly motivated to invest because they love and respect you, and hopeful that the investment will lead them, and you to a greater chance of success and wealth. It is up to you to look out for their interest, and do everything you can to ensure that they will not regret giving you money to get your enterprise off of the ground.

Even though personal money might be the easiest money for you to secure, you must be very careful about taking money from a friend or family member and diligent in ensuring (to the greatest degree possible) that the money will be used wisely and result in the kind of success for which both of you are hoping.

It is a risky game – certainly there is the potential of turning that small pot of private money into a larger pot of money. But if the venture fails you will have to deal with both a failed business enterprise AND substantial ill will from the personal friends and family whose money you lost in the efforts. Just be careful as you think of how much personal money to get and from whom to get it.

> The only time that personal money makes sense is in the very early stage of your enterprise when you can use a small sum of personal money to greatly increase the likelihood of getting much larger sums of money that will be critical to your ultimate success.

For example, it might be very helpful for you to have $10K-$50K of personal money: 1) to help offset the costs of securing government funding for early-stage product-development work, or 2) to build a professional-looking working prototype of your invention and finance a professional market-analysis study to convince private investors that there is a good business opportunity behind your invention. Indeed, some private investors will want to see that you already have a small pot of personal money devoted to the enterprise before they will consider investing more substantial sums of money in the enterprise. In other words, they will want to see that other people believe in you before they will believe in you! So, securing a modest amount of personal money up front can go a long way to proving your credibility to future investors.

Government Money – "good money"

The second category of working capital is money from the Federal and State governments, which is intentionally set aside for investment in small, product innovation companies like yours. Unlike most private-investment money, which will be discussed in the next section, most government money for small businesses does not come with *equity* strings attached.

In Chapter 4 I talked about how your Constitutional rights to protect and market your own ideas have been expanded upon in several key laws related specifically to the protection of patents, trade secrets, trademarks and copyrights. In the early 1980's, the Federal Government went one step further in promoting the development and protection of inventions within the small business sector by passing the Small Business Innovation Development Act and the Bayh-Dole Act.[36]   The Small

---

[36] *Research Administration and Management*, by Elliott C. Kulakowski and Lynne U. Chronister, Jones Bartlett Publishers, (2006), pp 628-638

Business Innovation Development Act created the *Small Business Innovation Research* (SBIR) Program and *Small Business Technology Transfer* (STTR) Program to provide funding for early-stage innovations that are too high risk for private investors. I briefly mentioned these programs in the last chapter, and will further discuss them in just a moment.

> The Federal and State governments provide money that can be used to fund your early stage product development work, and they will do so without requiring you to give up any substantial rights of ownership in your enterprise or your intellectual property! Now do you see why it is "good money?"

The second key piece of legislation, the Bayh-Dole Act sponsored by senators Birch Bayh of Indiana and Bob Dole of Kansas and enacted by Congress in 1980, provided for a major change in Government policy regarding intellectual property arising from Government-funded research. Specifically, the Act permits small businesses and universities that participate in the SBIR and STTR programs to maintain ownership of any inventions they develop under the programs, provided that the business discloses the invention to the Government prior to filing for a patent and grants the government the right to use the invention royalty free. The Bayh-Dole Act eliminated a 200-year-old Government policy that all intellectual property developed under any Government contract was the property of the Government. In doing so this key piece of Federal legislation, coupled with the Small Business Innovation Development Act, has provided financial assistance and intellectual-property ownership assurances that have launched thousands of small, product innovation businesses.

Both the SBIR and STTR programs are administered by the U.S. Government Small Business Administration (SBA),[37] and are aimed at stimulating growth and development of small, high-tech, product innovation businesses. Eleven Federal departments participate in the SBIR program, and five departments participate in the STTR program. Most of the SBIR and STTR awards come from the Department of

---

[37] http://www.sba.gov/SBIR/

Defense (DOD), the National Institutes of Health (NIH), the Department of Energy (DOE), the National Science Foundation (NSF), and the National Aeronautics and Space Administration (NASA). In total, the Federal Government awards over $2 billion annually to small high-tech businesses through these programs through approximately 5,000 new Phase I program awards and 2,000 new Phase II program awards.

Although the basic rules for the program are fairly uniform between the various Federal departments, the actual processes for implementing the program vary dramatically from department to department. In order to be successful in securing an SBIR or STTR grant, it is very important for the company to do some research on the particular Federal department(s) from which they are seeking money, and fine-tune their plans and proposals to best-fit the needs of that particular department. Fortunately, all of the departments post names of program managers on their SBIR/STTR Web pages, and these people provide good initial points of contact and valuable sources of information for any company who is new to the process.

One final point on the topic of government money is that most State governments also have a variety of programs to stimulate small-business development within the state including tax-incentives, low-cost loans, workforce grants to help offset the cost of hiring and training new staff members, etc. Information for these programs can usually be found through the Secretary of State's office, the Governor's office, or the State's Office for Economic Development. Although the amount of money available from the State government is not usually very great, it can be a worthwhile compliment to other financial resources you are securing to help your enterprise get moving.

Private-investment money – "bad money"

This brings us to the third category of working capital – private-investment money. This category includes money from venture capitalist, angel investors, investment bankers, etc. Every day, it is the money that makes many small and large businesses get off the ground, and it is the money that makes Wall Street work. Of course, private-investment money is, by definition, *personal money* – money from people. However, unlike money from your mother or your aunt, private investors are in the business of loaning working capital. So the nature of the money and the consequences of using the money are very different than the nature and consequence of using personal money from family and friends.

> Private-investment money can be thought of as "bad money." Not "bad" as in defective, harmful, or inferior, but rather "bad" as in the modern Generation-Y version of the word. This money is all business and comes from people who have steely eyes and are very driven to achieve personal financial success.

Unlike personal investors who want to help you and care little about your elevator pitch, private investors want to help themselves and will only help you if your elevator pitch defines an exciting and lucrative business opportunity for them. Can you associate with private investors and work with their money? Absolutely you can – people like you do it every day. To do so only requires that you have a compelling business story and that you understand the nature and the expectations of the people who might be investing it in your project, and work hard to meet their expectations.

There are a wide variety of sources of investment money that I am lumping together under this category of private-investment money. Although it is beyond the scope of this book to discuss all of these possible sources, I would like to further subdivide this category of money into two sub-categories in an effort to draw a fairly clean distinction that will help you better understand how to secure the money and what the potential investors might expect in return for their investments. These two sub-categories of private-investment money are: *credit* investment money and *equity* investment money. The differences between the sub-categories are explained below.

Credit investment money. If you have a car loan, a home mortgage, a credit card, or a student loan, you already have gone through the process of securing *credit investment money*. Indeed, credit investment money is essentially a loan – plain and simple. Like all other types of lending organizations, credit investors are in the business of giving out cash loans or lines of credit (access to cash reserves) in return for interest and principal payments over time. Like all other types of loans, business-investment loans from credit investors will require some collateral, which is oftentimes a partial (possibly greater than 50%) ownership in the business in the event that the business is unable to pay back the loan within the specified terms.

Typically, *credit investment* money comes with a higher interest rate than personal loans. In today's difficult credit market, interest rates of 15%-20% might not be unheard of! These high interest rates are a reflection of the risk that a credit investor is taking by investing in small-business enterprises. Of course, as with most business deals, striking a deal with a credit investor is a process of negotiation, and the stronger your business enterprise, the better the terms you will be able to negotiate in the deal. Finally, it is usually possible to structure a credit-investment agreement that includes options for you to buy back the business-ownership interest that you have posted as collateral for the loan in the event that you are able to pay off the loan earlier than planned.

Traditionally, the most common sources of credit investment money are investment-banking groups that specialize in financing business enterprises. Typically, these are larger banking organizations headquartered in major metropolitan areas – not personal banking businesses that you might find in your small hometown. However, your hometown banker probably knows about investment-banking groups that might serve your area, and could probably be a big help in starting your search for credit investment money, if you choose to seek out this type of money.

It is very unusual for credit investors to get involved in early-stage enterprises, as the risks are too great. So you should confine your consideration of credit investments to a point in time when your enterprise is off the ground and has an established and positive track record.

Equity investment money. If you own stock or mutual funds (either outright or through an Individual Retirement Account, IRA) then you are an *equity investor!* You have invested some of your money in someone else's business enterprise, and the essence of that agreement is fairly straightforward – if the business grows and makes money, your investment grows and you make money too! Of course, if the business falters or fails and the stock prices drop, then you lose some portion, or all of the money you invested.

Unlike credit investment money, which is financing a debt that your business either has or is planning to create, equity investment money is purchasing a portion of your business in return for some percentage ownership and some degree of control over the business.

Also unlike a loan, equity investment money traditionally doesn't require a standard payback schedule (i.e., monthly payments). Rather, equity investors are generally looking for "back-end" payments in the form of royalties, dividends, etc., and an option for the investor to sell back his or her ownership stake (or a portion thereof) at some time in the future.

There is a wide range of sources for equity investment money. Indeed, some investment–banking groups deal in both credit investments and equity investments. However, the most common sources of equity investment money are: 1) *venture capital groups* – businesses that sell interest in an equity-investment fund to shareholders and then invest that money in private enterprises like yours, and 2) *angel investment groups* – organizations of wealthy investors who collectively fund private enterprises. Arguably, the personal-investment money (4-F or "ugly" money) that you might have secured for your enterprise from an aunt or uncle is equity investment money, as they were granting you money up-front for some back-end stake in the enterprise. However, unlike personal money, private-investment money that you might get from a professional equity investment organization will come with very strict terms and conditions!

Possibly the biggest challenge in securing equity investment money is in opening a dialogue with potential investors. Unlike credit investment groups, which can be accessed through normal banking avenues, many equity-investment groups are less easy to access, and require some degree of *networking* – social interactions between you and the prospective investors. Venture capital groups are generally more structured and easy to approach than angel-investment groups, but both types of organizations intentionally tend to obscure their points of contact as a way of sifting through the large volume of requests for funding that they would otherwise be inundated with. If you want to better understand the nature of these private investors, you might consider reading: "The Millionaire Next Door,"[38] which does a nice job of exposing key common traits and practices among America's wealthy investors.

Persistence is key in developing a dialogue with either venture groups or angel groups. You can start to gain access into these private-investment organizations through civic groups like your local Chamber of Commerce, your state's Office of Economic Development, and/or private-investment societies in your area. Most importantly, you absolutely MUST have a crisp, accurate, and exciting elevator pitch in your hands when you make a contact with one of these organizations. Your first contact will be critical to your success in getting follow-on meetings, and ultimately in securing funding. You must also be persistent and professional in pursuing all contacts that you make – always bear in mind that there are another 10-20 people like yourself who might be talking with the same investors at the same time that you are talking with them. To secure private-investment money, you must sell yourself and make your business opportunity look more attractive than any other opportunity that the investors might be considering at the time.

Strategic partners – an alternative to late-stage equity investors

Before leaving the discussion of the different types of money that are available to you, I want to talk about another resource that could either bring money into your enterprise, or lessen the financial burden by sharing in some aspects of the later stages of your product-development effort. This resource is a *strategic partner* and their involvement might

---

[38] *The Millionaire Next Door: The Surprising Secrets Of Americas Wealthy,* by Thomas J. Stanley and William D. Danko, Pocket Publishers (1998)

include undertaking specific tasks, sharing risks, responsibilities, resources and most importantly sharing the eventual rewards of the successful enterprise.

> A *strategic partner* is a business partner who wants to work with you to accelerate or facilitate bringing your product to market and ensure its success through a hands-on involvement in the enterprise. In return for this involvement, the strategic partner will become an equity holder in your enterprise – either obtaining partial ownership of the business or exclusive rights to market and sell the products developed from the invention.

Usually, a strategic partner is a bigger, proven company that is already established in the target market for your invention. As such, they bring several capabilities that can help you save time, cost, and risk associated with bringing your product to the market. For example, let's say that you are developing a new software product but you don't have a mass distribution network established. You could develop a strategic partnership with an existing software-development company for distribution of your product. Such a partnership would be a "win-win" proposition if your product compliments, rather than competes with, other products they already distribute, and if the commission and fees that you might pay them are small in comparison to the expenses you would have incurred in developing your own distribution network.

Another potentially valuable strategic partner might be an established company who you have already identified as a possible competitor for your product. Indeed, the old adage: "if you can't beat them, join them," might be worth considering in this situation. As you look at the long road ahead of you to develop and market your product, and the potential that you will have an uphill battle to gain acceptance in the market, it might make perfectly good sense to consider creating an alliance with an existing company who would otherwise be a competitor.

Strategic partnerships through "open innovation." Fifty years ago, most product innovation companies made no attempt to work collaboratively with other companies through strategic partnering. Today for many reasons more and more companies have come to adopt a very different paradigm of proactively engaging strategic partners in a product innovation process that has become known as *open innovation*.[39] The central idea behind open innovation is that companies can become more successful in the long run if they compliment their in-house, product innovation research efforts with outside product innovation research from other companies. In the best-structured scenarios, these strategic partnerships result in two-way transfer of intellectual property: purchase of outside-developed IP from outside partners and sale of in-house-developed IP to outside partners.

Open innovation is most-rapidly gaining acceptance in the *high-tech* product innovation business sector – companies who are developing new products that involve a wide range of advanced technologies. One of the underlying reasons for this trend in high-tech product innovation businesses is that the new technologies are becoming so diverse that it is very difficult for any single business to remain at the forefront of all technologies that might bring value to their product lines. So open-innovation strategic partnerships between larger, high-tech product innovation companies and smaller, technology-development companies are rapidly becoming more popular. Some prominent large high-tech product innovation companies that are currently promoting open innovation include IBM, Nokia, and Procter & Gamble.

Finding the best strategic partnership. Regardless of whether your invention is high-tech or low-tech, your company and the right strategic partner can both enjoy benefits from an open collaboration. The keys to finding the right partnership are:

1. Find a partner who embraces the open innovation paradigm and has a record of working well with small businesses.

A simple first question to ask a potential partner is: "have you ever worked with a small business like ours before?" If the answer is: "no," you should probably keep looking!

---

[39] *Open Innovation: The New Imperative for Creating and Profiting from Technology*, by Henry Chesbrough, Harvard Business School Press, Boston (2003)

132

2. Create a "win-win" partnering agreement through which both companies benefit substantially from the partnership and are highly motivated to make the partnership work.

Always take the time to fully understand the "value proposition" to the partner – the financial benefit of the partnership and the product innovation you are offering through it. If you understand what they value in your product, you can always stay focused on providing that!

3. Work hard to build healthy, collaborative relationships at all levels with the partnering organization: the executive level (CEO to CEO), the senior management level, and down to the working level.

In the end, a strategic partnership is truly a partnership, which means that it works if everyone involved works at it. A relationship that only exists at the top will not succeed when the technical teams at the bottom fail to work together!

4. Define very specific goals and expectations for the joint project. Review progress against those goals regularly. And maintain a very active communication at all levels of connection between the organizations.

Just like any other relationship, this type of relationship requires constant management and very explicit dialogue over goals and expectations. Without this kind of engagement and common view of the future, the relationship is doomed.

For all of the potential up side of a strategic partnership, it should be clear that identifying the best strategic partner, defining a "win-win" partnering agreement, and developing the relationship is a very challenging and somewhat delicate proposition. In essence, you are opening yourself and your innovative product concept to prospective partnering companies that might view your invention as competitive with their established products. Assuming that the company is large, well established, and not sincerely interested in your product, they could easily seek to structure an agreement that allows them to shelve your product in favor of keeping their existing products in the forefront. This is a very real risk that you should always keep in the front of your mind as you explore any possible partnership.

Establishing these contacts, opening the dialogue, and building the relationship demands a great deal of care and caution. Always start your initial dialogue under the auspices of a "non-disclosure agreement" (NDA), which is a legal agreement that protects both you and the prospective partner from misuse of each other's proprietary information. Also develop a plan of engagement with prospective partners whereby you start the dialogue with basic discussion topics (e.g., "have you ever partnered with small businesses like us before?") that can serve to weed out the good from the bad partnering opportunities. Finally, be prepared to take a long time in developing the relationship and fully consider the business and legal consequences before actually signing a legally binding agreement.

> Just like in a marriage, be absolutely sure that the strategic partner you select is the right partner before you sign an agreement, and be absolutely committed to making the partnership work after you sign the agreement. If you do this you can expect to find the relationship to be rewarding and address not only your financial issues but also many of the technical issues that might otherwise have stalled out your efforts.

How much money do you need and which money is best for you?

Now you have a better idea of the different types of money and support through strategic partnerships that are available to help finance and move your enterprise forward. The next questions are: how much money ultimately do you and a prospective strategic partner need, and which type of money is best?

The total cost of bringing your invention to market – from early concept through all stages of product development, manufacturing scale-up, and distribution – can easily be in the range of $5M to $10M, depending on the complexity, production cost, and anticipated sales volume of the product. In fact, high-tech products that require government certification (e.g., medical devices, aerospace flight-vehicle components, etc.) can easily cost an additional $10M simply due to the lengthy certification testing programs that are necessary prior to market entry. Manufacturing scale-up alone can cost several million dollars due to capital equipment purchases necessary to set up a production line.

In most cases, you will not be able to, nor will you necessarily want to secure all of this money from a single source. Rather, your needs will most likely be best met through a capitalization plan that combines and leverages financial resources form several sources. So, you need to start developing a capitalization plan through which you will secure millions of dollars of investment capital from multiple sources, and you need to couple this plan closely with your marketing plan and your product-development plan in order for you to move your enterprise forward and ensure that your good ideas ultimately make it into the market.

Typical product-development and manufacturing scale-up program funding profile. Luckily, you don't need to have all of your money up-front, nor do you need to secure all of that money from a single source. Indeed, most start-up product innovation businesses secure their capital in three or four stages or increments. The following chart depicts a funding profile for a product-development program that lasts three years, and costs a total of $5M. The table details how this program might be divided into four phases, with top-level goals and total funding for each phase defined. The four program phases are representative of a typical step-by-step, milestone-based, product-development and manufacturing scale-up program as discussed in the last chapter.

This funding profile represents a relatively fast-paced product-development effort and I include it in order to make several key points about capitalization of your enterprise. The three-year timeframe and $5M total funding level are representative of a fairly aggressive development program for a product of average complexity and moderate cost (i.e., maybe $100 to $1,000 per unit production cost). Furthermore, I have estimated that about half of that total cost ($2.5M) will be consumed in the last phase of manufacturing scale-up and market insertion, which is consistent with a moderate initial production volume of roughly 10,000 to 50,000 units per year.

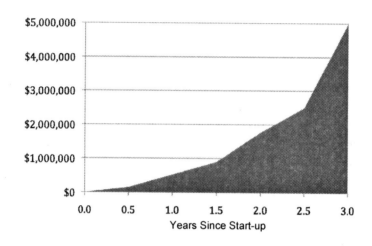

	Phase I	Phase II	Phase III	Phase IV
Time Duration	6 months	12 months	12 months	6 months
Total Funding	$150K	$750K	$1.6M	$2.5M
Top-Level Milestone(s) for the Phase	Proof-of-concept model and early market study	Design development and demonstration	Design-verification testing and pilot-scale manufacturing	Full-scale manufacturing, quality-acceptance testing, market insertion

Typical funding phases for $5M product-development program

During the "dot-com" explosion of the 1990's such fast-paced product-development enterprises became commonplace among so-called "ultrapreneurs".[40] Now investors tend to be more risk averse preferring longer development times, higher total funding levels, and more interim milestones to provide greater assurance for success. Of course, the actual budget for your enterprise will vary dramatically depending on complexity, cost, and production volume of your product.

---

[40] *Ultrapreneuring: Taking a Venture From Start-Up to Harvest in Three Years or Less,* by James B. Arkebauer, McGraw-Hill (1993)

Note that the spending rate of a product innovation program is typically modest at first ($150K in the first six months of this example), and accelerates rapidly as the product nears market insertion ($2.5M in the last six months of this example).

This spend-rate profile is reflective of the fact that, at first, your team will be relatively small and the total number and cost of prototypes that you build and test will be minimal. As the design matures and the extent of the testing program grows in order to address the entire array of design requirements your team will also grow and your spend rate will increase. In the final phases of the effort, your team might stay relatively constant in size, but you will see dramatic increases in expenses associated with purchase of capital equipment for setting up the manufacturing process. In Phase III, your capital equipment expenditures might be several hundred thousand dollars (~$200-500K) in order to achieve a *pilot-scale* (100-1,000 unit/year) production volume. Ultimately your capital equipment costs to achieve full production volume might be on the order of millions of dollars and will dominate the expenditures during Phase IV.

An example of a capitalization plan with multiple funding sources.
The third major point that I want to make is that the funding generally comes in increments of increasing quantity, which is consistent with an overall strategy of bringing multiple investors into the game at different points along the product-development path. If you are like many product innovation start-ups, you will kick-off your efforts with a modest first infusion of personal ("4-F") money – say $50K. Unless you have very deep pockets, or know someone who does, this first infusion will not even get you through the first proof-of-concept phase. You could very likely need a few hundred thousand dollars to get you through this phase, and this is a perfect place to consider securing a SBIR grant from the Federal government. Indeed, a typical Phase I SBIR grant will give you $100K of cash to spend on your proof-of-concept effort, and 9-12 months of time to spend it.

If you are diligent with your own money and the Phase I money that you might be able to get from the Federal Government, you might also expect to attract a Phase II SBIR grant as a follow-on to your Phase I grant, which would bring you an additional $750K of Government money over a two-year period after completion of the one-year Phase I effort. In total, the private money that you might have gotten from friends and family, plus a Phase I/II SBIR grant from the Federal Government will probably net you an amount approaching $1M – a sizeable sum but substantially less than your total-funding needs.

However, if you were successful in getting this personal and government money to launch your effort, and your early engineering-development and marketing efforts are on track, you are very likely in a good position to get a first round of private-investment money to take the project on through Phase II and into Phase III. Typically, angel investors will provide equity investments in the range of $200K-$1M for mid-stage startup companies – especially if the company has already secured some seed money from personal investors and/or the Federal Government. Venture capital groups usually invest in later-stage companies in the $1–4 million range, or greater. So this presents a nice scenario whereby you can consider angel funding to push you through Phase II and into Phase III, and VC funding or a strategic partner for additional investments to cover the balance of Phase III and all of Phase IV.

A key trait of this notional capitalization plan is that it is diversified by involving a range of investors each accepting a range of risk and investing in the enterprise at different stages.

The following chart depicts this funding strategy for the $5M program that was outlined previously. The four phases of the program are still shown horizontally in time, with the total funding profile (top line of the chart) is identical to that shown previously. In addition, this chart shows how the four sources of funding might overlay to build up the total funding profile that you need to secure. Finally, the accompanying table gives a breakdown of the total funding from each source and for each program phase. Again, these numbers are only estimates of a notional funding profile that might be built around this "average" product-development enterprise. However, they represent very realistic estimates of the levels of funding and the time sequencing of funding that are achievable from the various sources.

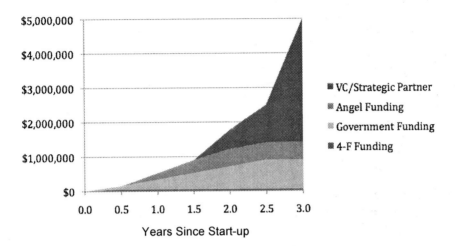

	Phase I	Phase II	Phase III	Phase IV	Total
Personal	$50K	$0	$0	$0	$50K
Government	$100K	$375K	$375K	$0	$850K
Angel Equity	$0	$375K	$125K	$0	$500K
VC Equity	$0	$0	$1,100K	$2,500K	$2,500K
Total	$150	$750K	$1,600K	$2,500K	$5,000K

Typical funding split and sequencing between different funding sources

Although this might seem to be a complicated solution to the problem of funding your enterprise, it is almost essential because no single investor, with the possible exception of personal investors who are very wealthy, will take on the total risk for such an enterprise. Indeed, you must develop a capitalization plan that has a diversity of investors and most importantly you must work to bring these investors onto your team in timely fashion that allows the product-development work to proceed and transition smoothly from phase to phase.

Bringing investors onto your team

As discussed in the last chapter, modern product innovation businesses generally follow a product-development program model that is built around specific developmental milestones and performance metrics. Indeed, the four-phase product-development program presented in the last subsection was constructed with a step-by-step, milestone-based framework in mind. In short, successful completion of a given phase requires two things: 1) the engineering-development team must meet the technical goals established for that phase, and 2) the business-development team must secure the funding for the follow-on phase. In this way, the engineering-development efforts are intimately coupled with the business-development and marketing efforts, and both efforts progress concurrently to ensure that the enterprise remains on track.

One can see then, that a critically important management function is to market the growing enterprise to the candidate investment communities sufficiently ahead of time, such that the increments of money will be available when the engineering-development team is in need of them. At the same time management must stay on top of the progress of the engineering-development team to ensure that the design is maturing in conformance with all of the requirements, and that the business opportunity defined in the elevator pitch is still valid.

"I was close to a breakthrough when the grant money ran out."

> One of the most tragic scenarios you could encounter is that you fail to secure follow-on funding despite meeting technical goals. If this happens, the team that you have worked hard to assemble will vanish and with it your likelihood of success will evaporate.

Understanding what the investors want. In Chapter 1, I briefly discussed the Entrepreneurial Standards Forum, which has developed a series of online tools for entrepreneurs and investors to assess the risk of any particular business enterprise.[41] I also recommended that you visit their website, fill out their survey, and read the reports that are generated. If you already did this, now is a great time to revisit and update your survey with the insights that you have gained to this point in the book. In essence, the survey is structured to help you define a "success path" that your business can take forward and tell you where you are on this path. The survey is also structured to give potential investors valuable feedback about the risk of investing in your enterprise. If you understand how investors might use this survey you are well on your way to understanding the most-critical issues that well-informed investors will consider before investing in your enterprise.

With this bit of background, let me now revisit the two categories of investors that you might seek out to seed your early-stage work – personal investors and government investors. Fortunately, these investors are the least demanding of all and the most willing to accept a high degree of risk that the enterprise will fail. Indeed, as discussed earlier, the Government SBIR program was originally conceived as a means to bridge the gap that exists between personal seed funding and mid-stage private funding opportunities. Through this wonderful program, the Government essentially provides a modest amount of money to worthy people with good ideas and with no expectation that the money will be paid back directly to the government.

However, the expectations of private-equity investors and strategic partners are much different. Both want to see up-front that you can give them a healthy rate of return on their investment. Furthermore, they will demand numerous contractual obligations that will help them minimize their risk and gain a certain degree of control over your

---

[41] http://es2f.org/

enterprise. One very typical contractual clause that might be required by a private investor is to allow the investor, or investment group, to be represented by one or more voting members of the Board of Directors of your company.

> Probably the most important (and valuable) aspects of personal and Government money for seeding a startup enterprise, is that neither source of money demand an equity stake in the enterprise, so you can use the money and still retain full control and ownership.

In general, early-stage investments represent a greater risk to the private-equity investor. Because of this, early-stage investors generally will demand a greater rate-of-return on their investment, and they will only be willing to invest money up to a certain limit in order to manage their risk of loss. Angel investors usually bear extremely high risk and seek investments that have the potential to return at least 10 or more times their original investment within 5 years, which represents an annual rate of return of approximately 60%! So in the scenario presented, the $500K of angel-investment money is coming in with an expectation that the company will generate sufficient revenues in the first 2-3 years of product sales to return as much as $5M back to these investors! To this end, these angel investors will often demand a defined exit strategy, such as plans for an *initial public offering* – conversion of ownership to public ownership through the offering of stock purchases – or a corporate acquisition during the first few years the product is in the market as a means to generate the required return on their investment

The later-stage, venture capital (VC) investors have a more modest, but still aggressive, expectation on their rates of return. A typical return rate for VC money would be between 25% and 50% per year - better than the average return from the stock market, but not as aggressive as angel investors might be seeking. Similar to the angel investors, a typical later-stage VC investment agreement will include a well-defined exit strategy that is oftentimes best met through a plan to sell the enterprise to a larger corporation or through an initial public offering. In some scenarios, VC investors will accept a guaranteed dividend, royalty stream or percentage of gross sales in combination with an option to sell back (i.e., liquidate) their investment at a point in the future. In either scenario, it is typical for VC money to remain tied up in the enterprise for 2-3 years, which means that the total cash-out for the investors could be on the order of *four times* their initial investment. So the $3.6M of VC funding that was included in the $5M product-development program example previously outlined would need to generate roughly $15M in payback on that investment.

> The harsh cold fact of building your enterprise using private-equity money is that you can only expect to attract that money if your enterprise has a very promising opportunity to turn into something that is very profitable in just a few years.

For the example I outlined, I assumed that a total of $4.1M of the $5M cost to market would come from a combination of angel equity investments and VC equity investment spread out mostly over the last two years of the product-development program. To attract these investments, your enterprise would have to become profitable such that it could return a total of roughly $20M within the first 2-3 years after product entry, either through royalties, dividends (profit sharing), or outright sale of the enterprise to a larger company or through an initial public offering. If these numbers sound astronomical, they are - especially to someone who might be new to the world of product innovation businesses. However, these are the kinds of numbers that your business must be capable of achieving, if you are to attract the level of private-investment money that you might need to be successful.

At this point, I want to bring your attention back to the concept of the elevator pitch. Now, you should see more clearly what must be conveyed in this brief, two-minute summary of your enterprise. Not only do you need to explain the product, the customer, the market, etc., but *also, most importantly*, you need to explain your entire capitalization plan, and the revenue model that you see developing in the first few years that the product is in the market. Without these key bits of information, there is no way for a private-equity investor to give your opportunity serious consideration. They are in the business of making money with their own money, and they are very skilled and adept at "sniffing out" good business opportunities. If your elevator pitch misses out on any of the key questions that were outlined earlier, they will see you as immature and too risky to even consider regardless of how exciting or clever your invention might be.

Finally, I want to discuss briefly the expectations that a strategic partner might have in joining your team. In general, strategic partners also have aggressive goals for the return on their investment, but they do not necessarily expect these goals to be met through direct payback from your enterprise within just a few years. For example, a strategic partner who is interested in marketing and distributing your invention will usually base their return-on-investment expectations on estimates for the amount of new revenues they will develop (i.e., new market capture) with your invention.

> In general, strategic partners tend to be more reasonable in their expectations for rate of return on their investment because they tend to have a longer time frame in mind during which they will benefit from the investment.

Whereas private-equity investors are usually looking for an opportunity to "get rich quick" (i.e., cash out within 3-5 years), strategic partners are usually looking for a stable, yet healthy, return over a longer period of time (i.e., 5-10 years). For this reason, bringing a strategic partner onto your team demands a very intimate discussion about their long-term business goals with your product, and their short-term financial expectations.

Securing the money. I opened this chapter with a relatively famous quote from the movie *Jerry Maguire*. If you haven't seen that movie, it is about the trials and tribulations of a sports agent (Jerry) who is working tirelessly to secure a new contract and higher pay for a football-player client. Through it all, the athlete remains completely ignorant of the business-side issues of the negotiations. Preferring instead to cede all responsibility for dealing with these issues to his agent, Jerry, and challenging Jerry with his simple, but solid expectation:

"Jerry - I want you to say it with meaning, brother! . . . Show me the money!"

I cited this quote because, at the end of the day, your enterprise needs money, and you need to be absolutely determined to secure this money through whatever means are necessary. If you don't have the desire or ability to secure the money yourself, then you must enlist the support of people who can and will perform this task. Indeed, it might be essential to consider using an agent or multiple agents to help in your efforts to secure money.

In order to secure Government funding, you might consider the services of a wide array of government-contracting specialty companies or consultants. There are many such organizations around the Washington DC metro area, as well as near the Federal laboratories that participate in the SBIR and STTR programs. In order to secure private-investment money, you might consider hiring a CEO who is already established with a track record of building product innovation businesses with your target market. If you are considering structuring a strategic partnership, then you absolutely must engage the services of a well-qualified business-transaction attorney who can understand your strategic goals and review/draft a strategic agreement that best meets those goals.

> In addition to considering agents to help you secure funding for your enterprise, you should plan to spend a year or more pursuing each funding source before you can expect to see each new increment of money.

Certainly, the involvement of agents on your behalf can shorten that time somewhat, but even the best well-connected and educated agent will require several months to start from scratch and sell a new enterprise to an interested investor.

Summary

To my astonishment, I have met many inventors and inexperienced entrepreneurs who truly believe that they can be successful with a good idea simply by *working hard*, and without having the benefit of *working cash!* It's an almost noble mentality. But sadly, in the product innovation business sector, hard work alone is not likely to lead to success. If you learned nothing else from Chapter 5, you learned that a proper product-development and manufacturing scale-up program (i.e., one that you can be reasonably sure will succeed) could be complex and costly.

If you learned nothing else from the present chapter, hopefully you learned that raising money to finance this product-development program is just as essential as having a solid program plan. Moreover, I hope that this chapter has also helped to unravel the mysteries that might have been vexing you about this very important piece of the puzzle. If so, then you now see that there are many resources available to you to further your education on the subject, and to ultimately help you become successful in securing the funding that your young enterprise needs to move forward.

It all starts with a solid business opportunity and a concise elevator pitch that explains this opportunity to potential investors and strategic partners. Beyond that, the main ingredient is persistence on your part and a thoughtful use of advisors or agents who are more adept than you at the art and science of marketing your enterprise to investors and strategic partners. Follow this formula and you will find that raising the money isn't as difficult as it might have seemed at the outset. With a solid capitalization plan in place and multiple lines of funding secured you are now ready to learn about the last piece of *The Inventor's Puzzle* – how to build the team that will actually develop your product and bring it into the marketplace.

7

The Team: An Introduction to Building a Successful Organization

"No man is an island entire of itself; every man is a piece of the continent, a part of the main; if a clod be washed away by the sea, Europe is the less, as well as if a promontory were, as well as any manner of thy friends or of thine own were; any man's death diminishes me, because I am involved in mankind. And therefore never send to know for whom the bell tolls; it tolls for thee."

– John Donne

John Donne's famous meditation, "No man is an Island," provides me the launching point for this chapter dealing with the final piece of *The Inventor's Puzzle* – building the organization to develop your product and bring it to the market. The central message within Donne's meditation is simply that all people are interconnected and reliant on one another for their existence. By now you appreciate that to be successful in a product innovation business, you cannot be *an island, entire of yourself.*

The world of product innovation business is a living example of John Donne's sociological theme. Many other people (e.g., investors, strategic partners, program managers, and product-development engineers) are critically important to your success.

Unfortunately, I have met many bright inventors who have chosen to go it alone for a number of reasons like protecting their ideas from piracy and minimizing the cost necessary to develop their ideas. Although I fully respect these motivations, I firmly believe, and now you also realize that there are other ways to address these issues while opening the door for the right team to help develop and market your product.

This chapter will be devoted to dissecting the organization that you will need to assemble to launch your enterprise. I will start the discussion by taking a step back and, with the new insights that I have built in the last four chapters, looking at the entire enterprise that you are considering from beginning to end. This complete view of the enterprise will help define the range of talent that you need to bring into your team and the time sequence in which you need to bring that talent on board. Then, I will talk about how you might use outside help to both recruit the right talent and also to fill gaps in your team. Finally, I will look at the makeup of the team by addressing two basic questions: 1) what does this team need to look like?; and 2) what is your role in building the team, as the inventor and/or lead protagonist of the effort?

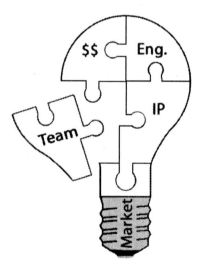

Building the team – the final piece of The Inventor's Puzzle.

Ultimately, my goal in this chapter is to help you better define the key members of your team, and to help you establish priorities for how to move forward in securing the right people for the team. I will not tell you much about the tactics of recruiting (posting job ads, conducting interviews, etc.). Rather, I want to focus this chapter on defining the strategic aspects of your recruiting efforts and some of the intangible qualities that you are seeking in the various team members in order to ensure that, collectively, they blend together and harmonize around the common purpose of making your enterprise a successful one.

A first view of the entire enterprise

By now, you have begun to gain a glimpse into the possible size and complexity of the enterprise that would be necessary to bring your invention to market. From a financial perspective, the last chapter explained that the product-development and manufacturing scale-up efforts could easily take several years and cost several million dollars. Also in the last chapter, you learned that it could take at least a year to secure your first infusion of operating capital to launch the enterprise. Finally, in the last chapter I talked briefly about a several-year time frame *after market entry* during which you will build up sales revenues or sell your company outright (through an IPO or merger/acquisition) and pay back private investors who provided you operating capital for the later-stage product-development activities.

> Most product innovation businesses are multi-year, multi-million dollar enterprises (or projects within a larger business) that must grow and evolve along with the evolving product.

Also by definition, the organization that will be assembled around the business enterprise will need to be capable of a wide variety of tasks. Of course, marketing and sales will ultimately be the key to gaining a return on your investment. However, leading up to the point of market entry, you will have a dedicated product-development team to refine the product design and a manufacturing and production team to actually put the product into production. Along the way you will be engaging private investors who have a vested interest in overseeing the enterprise, and you might find that you will also engage other outside advisors who might bring specific skills, network contacts, and insights to bear in helping your enterprise succeed.

So what will this organization look like? How many people will it employ? How will it be structured? Of course, there is no way to answer these questions definitely without carefully considering the specific product you are developing and the marketing issues you will have to face. However, there are some basic issues that are common to all product innovation businesses and that can help you better understand what the organization will look like and how big it might become in time.

A notional organizational chart. There are several intrinsically important functions that need to be performed by the organization if it is to be efficient and successful in transforming an invention into a marketable product. The following picture provides a notional *organizational chart* – a graphical depiction of the organization that divides key functions and responsibilities into critical positions or groups of positions, and that defines some of the critical lines of communication between these positions or groups. This organizational chart is not meant to be absolute, but rather it is intended to help you better understand how the critical functions within the organization will be divided between key management/leadership positions and how several distinct teams of individuals, who are actually doing the hard work of developing manufacturing and selling the products, will be managed and interconnected.

Indeed, the organization that must be built will be a "team of teams," each with complimentary roles, and some internal to the company and some external to the company. In the middle of this organizational chart is the most-critical position to the enterprise – the *Chief Executive Officer (CEO)* – the person who is most-centrally responsible for the success or failure of the entire enterprise. I will discuss the CEO's role in more depth in a later section, but at this point I will just say that, in the spirit of Harry S. Truman, this person should have a plaque on his desk that says: "The Buck Stops Here!"

Two of the CEO's key roles are: 1) to bring money into the enterprise to allow the product to be launched, and 2) to ensure that the product offering ultimately returns money on that investment.

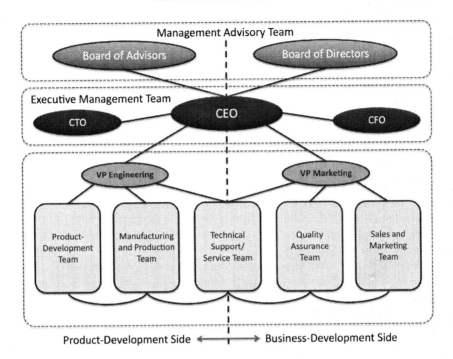

Product-Development Side ←——→ Business-Development Side

A notional organizational chart for a product innovation business.

Working intimately with the CEO will most likely be two or three other senior executive managers, whose responsibilities will cover areas of strategic concern to the enterprise. For example, issues related to the intellectual property holdings of the company might be overseen by a *Chief Technology Officer (CTO)*, issues related to business finances might be overseen by the *Chief Financial Officer (CFO)*, and issues related to the internal operations of the company might be overseen by a *Chief Operations Officer (COO)*. Alternatively, some or all of these functions might be absorbed by the CEO or other senior-level managers, depending on the size of the enterprise and the amount of effort needed to address each strategic issue.

This *Executive Management Team* will interact periodically with several outside review bodies. Usually, a formal *Board of Directors*, which is comprised of a combination of business experts in the market of interest and private investors, will interact with the CEO on a monthly or quarterly basis. In the case of publically owned and many privately owned companies, the CEO actually works for the Board of Directors. So there is a fiduciary responsibility to uphold in this relationship in addition to an advisory-executive responsibility.

Also many small companies will create a *Board of Advisors* who hold no particular fiduciary responsibility but who have some insights into either the technologies being packaged in the product or the market and customer base. Finally, many CEO's will also create *ad hoc* – narrowly focused on a particular topic – relationships with outside consultants and other business leaders in order to further ensure their success. You might recall from earlier, that I said a key trait of most successful CEO's in the product innovation business sector is a very outgoing personality and a social approach to the business. Well, the engagement of one or more outside advisors and boards is a manifestation of this quality.

> All effective CEO's delegate and share responsibilities among an executive management team that consists of internal executives (e.g., COO, CTO, CFO, etc.) and external advisors and directors. If properly balanced, this team efficiently addresses both the tactical (i.e., day-to-day) issues and the strategic (i.e., long-term planning) issues that inevitably arise.

Within the company a Vice President of Engineering or a COO often oversees engineering and manufacturing teams, whereas a Vice President of Marketing or a VP for Business Development oversees the marketing and sales teams. Under each of these senior management positions will be teams of people with common focus and a degree of interaction and cross-teaming communication. In the notional organizational chart, I have suggested five teams, two under each VP, with a fifth team responsible for technical support and service functions reporting to either or both VPs. This partitioning of responsibilities at the team level is only notional and provided just to illustrate how teams might be built around a specific task area.

Finally, I have also included a vertical line in the organizational chart that roughly divides the organization into a "business-development half" and a "product-development half." I include this line, not to suggest a hard separation between those two functions. Indeed, as I have discussed at great length, the people who are responsible for marketing *MUST* be in close communication with those who are doing the product engineering! Rather, I include this division within the company to point out a *right-brain versus left-brain* dynamic that will exist within your organization, and create some tension between the more structured engineering (*left-brain*) side and the more creative marketing and sales (*right-brain*) side.

In general, the engineering teams will feel a bit at odds with the marketing and sales teams, and vice versa. The tension is rooted in the fact that engineering teams tend to be more focused on the technical aspects of the design whereas the marketing and sales team tend to be more focused on features that they see as critical to making the sale (e.g., the product image). Two very important parts of the organization that will bridge the gap between the engineering and marketing teams are the *Quality Assurance Team* and the *Technical Support and Service Team*. The Quality Assurance Team is ultimately held responsible for ensuring that the final product meets all requirements established in a consistent and repeatable fashion. The Technical Support and Service Team is the organization that "lives" with the customer after the product is sold and provides customer service in support of the product.

> The inherent tension between engineering and marketing can be a very helpful driving force that ultimately leads to a final product that is a healthy compromise including features that are most easily achievable by the engineering team and features that are most easily marketable by the sales team.

If properly structured, both of these teams can serve an internal "police force," and arbiter between marketing and engineering – negotiating revisions to requirements, and establishing inspection and acceptance standards to verify that products coming off of the production line live up to the customers' expectations. In the notional organizational chart, I have shown the Technical Support and Service Team as reporting to both the VP of Engineering and the VP of Marketing, whereas the Quality Assurance Team reports to the VP of Marketing alone. In some organizations this team would reside under the VP of Engineering, but in my experience, the function is better aligned with the responsibilities of the VP of Marketing.

How big will your organization be? In total, your enterprise could extend for many years, consume millions of dollars, and involve dozens, or even hundreds of people! Indeed, your business will grow in proportion to the business opportunity. If your invention is a good one and your business opportunity is strong – meaning that you will be selling a large number of your products, your business will grow large accordingly. How can you estimate, and begin planning for, the number of employees your business will need? Well, there are two key considerations that will ultimately determine this aspect of your business: 1) *annual revenues* – the amount of money that your business will generate per year, and 2) *in-source versus out-source of critical functions* – your strategy as to which functions you will keep within the business and which functions you will send outside of the business via subcontracts, vendor agreements, and/or strategic partnerships.

Revenue-Based Estimate of Company Size. In the last chapter, I presented a notional three-year funding plan for a moderate-sized product-development business. Indeed, this funding plan was constructed using some basic assumptions as to the complexity of the product, and the number of people who would be necessary to advance it through the various phases of the product-development program. For a business at this phase of its growth, the staff is primarily composed of engineers, skilled technicians, and professional marketing and business-development people. For the most part, these highly trained professionals will be salaried employees commanding an average annual salary of say $75K with significant employment benefits.

> A rough rule of thumb for estimating the gross annual operating budget of a product-development company is two times the total salary expenses that are paid by the company.

So, a product-development company comprised of ten employees who draw an average salary of $75K would need an operating budget of approximately $1.5M per year in order to satisfy the payroll and benefits of the employees, and also to have a reasonable working budget for purchase of equipment, subcontracts, rent, and other corporate overhead expenses. If I apply this $150K/employee-year factor, it is possible to derive a rough estimate for the number of employees needed at each phase of the three-year product-development program outlined in the last chapter. The accompanying chart shows the three-year funding profile that was presented in the last chapter with an estimate for the number of employees at the company during each phase of the program. As you would imagine, the company can and must grow as you move the product into successive, and more costly, phases of its development.

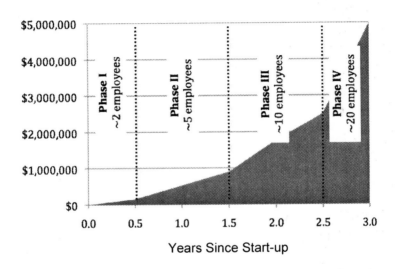

	Phase I	Phase II	Phase III	Phase IV
Time Duration	6 months	12 months	12 months	6 months
Total Funding	$150K	$750K	$1.6M	$2.5M
Approximate # of employees	2	5	10-11	20

Estimated number of employees during each phase of a notional, $5M, four-phase product-development program

The Effect of Outsourcing Key Functions. The other key consideration that will affect the size of your company is your strategy on which functions to keep within the company and which to *outsource* – move outside of the company through subcontract, vendor agreements, and/or strategic partnerships. Of course, outsourcing still costs you money because you still have to generate the revenues necessary to pay for this function. However, outsourcing saves you from having to hire permanent employees to perform those functions. In situations where the functions are either *short-lived* – only required for a short duration of time – or not within your company's *core competence* – the collection of functions that your staff is particularly adept at performing – outsourcing might be a very good option for your company.

One very specific example of outsourcing is a strategic partnership through which you connect your company with a larger more established company for manufacturing, sales, and distribution of your product. I discussed this type of strategic partnership in the last chapter as a means through which you could minimize the need for late stage private-investment money. Indeed, this type of a partnering agreement has the dual benefit of reducing your capitalization needs and reducing your hiring/staffing needs. To further illustrate the concept, the following picture depicts a version of the organizational chart presented earlier with the manufacturing, technical support, quality assurance, and sales and marketing functions grouped together and outsourced to a strategic partner.

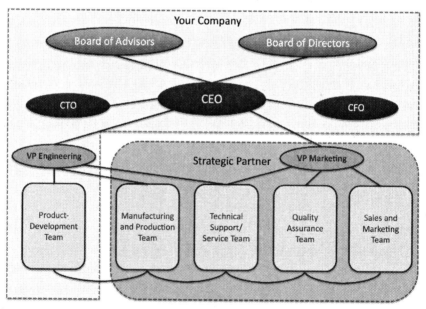

An organizational chart in which the production, support, marketing and sales functions are outsource to a Strategic Partner

The essential ingredients for successful teams

Every successful new product that is brought to the market is the result of a combined effort on the part of many people. Indeed, without such a team in place, I firmly believe that failure is almost a *fait accompli* – a foregone conclusion. In this section, I want to focus on the portion of your team that will be internal within your company – your staff of employees.

> Just as a successful sports team is much more than a collection of talented people, a successful product innovation team is highly synergistic, interdependent, multidisciplinary, complimentary, and interconnected in such a way that, as a collective, it can and does efficiently cross over the numerous and unavoidable barriers to entry into the market.

Bear in mind that no two teams will ever be precisely the same in size or makeup. Of course, the breadth of talent that is required and the arrangement of teams that allows those talented people to perform their jobs most efficiently will depend heavily on the nature of the product you are developing. For simple products that utilize straightforward designs and engineering technologies, the teams might be relatively small. For complex, high-tech products, the teams might be larger and the key leaders on those teams might be nationally recognized experts in the critical areas of technology. Regardless of these variations, I have found that all successful teams share some traits and qualities in common, which I will try to expose here.

A common sense of purpose – an esprit de corps. All organizations exist around a common purpose. Without it, the organization is meaningless. With it, the organization can become powerful and purposeful in its efforts. In a small, product innovation company, the common purpose might seem obvious – to develop the product and get it into the market. However, that shared purpose alone might not be sufficient to fully catalyze the creative talents and energies among your team, and direct those energies such that the team moves forward efficiently and in the direction that is most certain to lead to success.

A common business goal that does not excite some level of *buy-in* - personal motivation – in the members of the product-development team, is not likely to be pursued aggressively by the team. To establish this personal drive you must be able to see the business opportunity from the perspective of each team member, and you must provide each member with the personal motivation that if the business enterprise succeeds they also succeed.

> A common business goal that provides each individual on the team with the potential of personal reward (both financial and professional) will create a high level of personal motivation and will naturally bread an *esprit de corps*.

More importantly, each team member's personal drive must be symbiotic with the personal drive in the other members. In other words, one person's personal success can't come at the price of another person's failure. If you are successful in creating this collective drive, you will have created a powerful sense of common purpose – *an esprit de corps* – and a collection of team members who see the team's success as a means for them to become personally successful, and vice versa.

Internal communication and collaboration. In the same way that no business leader is an "island," no member of a product innovation team can be an "island," working in isolation from the remainder of the team. In my career of research and product development, I have consistently found that one of the most critical elements of successful teams is the element of internal communication and collaboration. Indeed, a critical function for any team leader is to instill in all team members a sense of responsibility for cooperation and communication.

> A culture of open dialogue and interaction breads ideas that are the byproduct of collaborative thought and are far superior to most ideas that emerge from the isolated thoughts of any single individual.

Teamwork and problem solving skills. Moving your invention from concept to market-ready product is, if nothing else, an exercise in problem solving. Just as I have cast this entire book under the metaphor of a puzzle, you will find that the daily challenges of advancing the product bring about an almost never-ending series of puzzles to be solved. This is the very essence of what is meant when I describe this kind of business enterprise as a "product innovation" business. You are literally trying to bring something new to the market, the details of which have never been addressed by other businesses nor have the features of the design become established in any other product. Hence, the team needs to communicate well and to have the array of talent and skill that is necessary to solve the breadth of problems it may encounter and the desire to use that array of talent cooperatively.

> Ultimately the team will be asked daily to solve problems, many that you can't anticipate and most that you couldn't envision a solution for if you could anticipate them. The measure of the team's success is then, quite simply, its ability to collectively study and solve hard problems through a combination of individual talent and creativity and a collaborative approach of teamwork and sharing of responsibility.

Opportunity for individuals to shine. Ultimately, any highly talented team is comprised of highly talented individuals, who, by their nature, seek to achieve a certain degree of personal success. You absolutely need talented people within your team, and as much as you need them to work together as a team, you also need to allow for the most talented among them to excel and shine in a way that their personal success doesn't threaten the remainder of the team. The best way for you to achieve this balance of personal drive with collective drive, is to avoid having two people whose roles are so similar and overlapping that either of them excelling might cause the other to become discouraged.

If you are a sports fan you immediately recognize that all sports teams are constructed in this way. Furthermore, the role of the coach or manager of that team is to make sure that everyone on the team is an expert at their position and wants to win personally, which sets the team up to win!

> Work hard to find unique positions on the team for each of the team players, and work harder to define the ways in which each player interacts with the others such that their skills and talents compliment each other rather than threaten each other.

The role of the CEO in building the team

At the top of any successful business is a person whose title is *Chief Executive Officer (CEO)*. The title includes the word "Executive" because her main responsibility is to ensure that the company *executes* on is business mission. In the case of a small, product innovation business that is endeavoring to turn new inventions into marketable products, the CEO is the person who, ultimately, is responsible for each of the top-level issues discussed previously in Chapters 3-6, as well as the topic of the present chapter – building the team. So to understand the makeup of a successful product-development and marketing team, it is best to first understand the makeup of that team's leader – the CEO.

One of the most popular and, in my opinion, finest business books that "dissect" CEOs of successful corporations is *Good to Great*, by Jim Collins.[42] If you are truly interested in understanding the makeup and personality traits of the most-successful CEOs, then I highly encourage you to read this book. For the purpose of our discussion here, I want to extract a few key attributes in an effort to help you better understand the type of person who should lead your efforts forward, as well as the means by which this person will build and maintain the team that will actually do the work!

In his book, Jim Collins defined a *Level 5 leader* as a person who achieves extraordinary success in the role of CEO through a very surprising combination of humility and resolve. Unlike the stereotypical corporate CEO who drives the ship with an iron fist and larger-than-life personality (Ted Turner's name comes to mind), Collins' research concluded that the most effective and successful CEOs are behind-the-scenes people who believe that the success of the organization depends more on the rest of the team than on themselves. This self-effacing leadership mentality might be unusual in the high-stakes world of corporate America, but Collins showed that it is typical of the most successful corporations.

People who actually live up to the description of a Level 5 leader are rare in the business world because the challenges of being a corporate CEO usually draw in people who are anything but self-effacing! So is it essential that such an individual manage your team? Maybe not, after all there are many successful CEOs who would say, "pooh-pooh" (or maybe more offensive things) to Jim Collins' theories. Nevertheless, understanding the mentality of a Level 5 leader is very helpful to better appreciate the challenges of building the proper team.

Without digressing further, let me cut to the chase and paraphrase here some of the key qualities of Level 5 leadership defined by Jim Collins and that are important to the effective product innovation CEO:

---

[42] *Good to Great: Why Some Companies Make the Leap--and Others Don't*, by James C. Collins, Harper Business (2001)

> The CEO must realize that the team is the organization's greatest asset – especially in preparing for the unknown challenges that lie ahead. By building the right combination of skills and encouraging the right inter-communications within the team, the CEO knows that he is setting the organization up for success.
>
> The CEO must also spend a lot of time getting the right people "on the bus," and the wrong people "off the bus." Furthermore, they appreciate each individual's strengths, weaknesses, and passions, and work to help them find the right "seat on the bus." Once, the team is properly in place, the CEO then must determine the direction to "drive the bus."

The metaphor of a bus is pretty commonly used in describing the team-building process, and it works to a point. However, it is also important to realize (as a Level 5 leader certainly does), that the team members are not just *passengers on a bus* (i.e., passive members in the organization). Rather, when properly selected, each of the team members is very active, and compliments the other members in ways that might be difficult to identify *a priori* – ahead of time. So just as in building a winning sports franchise, this is the very essence of leadership and team building that is necessary for the kind of small, creative, successful product innovation organization that will evolve your invention into a marketable product.

The inventor's role on the team

What is the inventor's role in building the team and in participating with the team as it moves the enterprise forward? Well, I hate to cop out here, but it is really up to him to help determine that role. Be careful, I am not giving the inventor *carte blanche* to define a position of royalty that best feeds his ego. Rather, I am saying that he should best know his own personal strengths and weaknesses, and he are in the best position to thoughtfully decide how he best fits into, and helps out, the organization.

Many inventors think that since they came up with the product idea, they are best fit to be the leader (CEO) of the organization that will turn the invention into a product. Well, if you are the inventor, you have to ask yourself if you have the experience, personality qualities, and wherewithal to effectively execute on all of the responsibilities of the CEO that I outlined in the last section? If you are like most inventors who are clever enough to have created the invention in the first place but not experienced in the product innovation business world, the odds are pretty good that you are NOT the right person to be the CEO of your own company. Unfortunately for many inventors, this humbling realization is hard to accept and any position in the organization other than the CEO seems like a demotion.

Well, if you are an inventor and are stumbling a bit with this idea, let me help you see it from a different perspective. Do you remember the children's parable: "The Emperor has no clothes?" If you don't, then I heartily encourage you to go buy a copy and read it to yourself. Furthermore, I would highly recommend that after each and every morning shower you stand naked in front of the mirror and fully apprise yourself of every wart, pimple, wrinkle, and fat bulge. Then imagine that, as the emperor of your enterprise, the LAST thing that you want to happen is for the rest of the organization to see you naked – literally or figuratively!

Is that a powerful enough analogy for you? If it isn't then you have never witnessed the utter embarrassment of an inventor and passionate "emperor" over a new product innovation company who simply doesn't know where or how he fits into the organization. The inventor must decide what he wants most out of the enterprise: a successful business or a personal learning experience on how to make a business fail? This is a tough pill to swallow for most bright, and entrepreneurial inventors. Certainly there are many inventors who can lead organizations and who do have the insights, experiences, and skills to be an effective CEO. But I am saying, with some level of conviction, that if you haven't done it before, it's probably not the right role for you.

> The inventor's central leadership role at the moment of conception and during the early stages of startup is clear. However, any inventor who lacks first-hand experience in product innovation business should see their central leadership role evolve to a supporting role while making room for an experienced CEO to drive the enterprise forward more efficiently and effectively.

" Hey look. The company president is butt naked! "

What does the inventor bring to the organization that nobody else in the organization brings to the table? Well, for starters, and harkening back to the message I delivered in Chapter 1, I contend that the inventor is, by definition, the source and center for the vision and passion that drives the effort forward. Never lose sight of this very essential ingredient. The best of organizations with the best of leadership STILL need to feed off of the passion and vision of a common purpose. Generally, the one who invented the idea is, *ipso facto*, the best person to maintain that passion and vision.

If you are both an inventor and experienced business leader, then you might very effectively take on the role of CEO and use that office to bring your passion and vision to the team. If you are only an inventor and lack the experience of a business leader, then your first and foremost role in building the team is to find the person who can be an effective CEO, and develop a relationship with him or her that sets you both up for success.

> A good CEO will appreciate the value of the inventor's passion and vision, and will want the inventor to be involved in such a way as to best capitalize on this passion and vision. At the same time, a good CEO will not want to give up critical corporate responsibilities to someone who is not experienced and capable of handling those responsibilities. Indeed, a good CEO would be precisely the one person in the room who would alert the inventor to the fact that he has "no clothes" – no role in that particular situation.

At the outset it will be up to the inventor to begin seeing beyond the cleverness of her invention and having the vision to see the business opportunity that it may bring. Even before she finds a CEO to actually take the reigns of your emerging enterprise, she must be the one who constructs the elevator pitch, which succinctly defines the motivation that will drive the enterprise forward. Her passion for the opportunity and her firm belief in the potential success will be the quality that attracts the right CEO candidate to her side.

After this relationship is established, it will continue to be her passion that will help create the internal esprit de corps, the buy-in from outside investors and strategic partners, and the excitement in the customer base that will drive them to buy her product instead of the other products offered by the competition. Ultimately, she should maintain this passion as a critically needed resource for her enterprise, but she should also work closely with her chosen CEO to refine her position in the organization over time in such a way that she will always been seen as a leader and driving force, and not as a naked emperor.

Connecting with the outside world – Enterprise 2.0?

Let me now shift the discussion from the internal makeup of your team to another topic of importance – the connections between your team and the outside world. These connections are multiple and range in scope from information gathering to technical collaboration. Regardless of the nature of the external connection, each one is potentially critical to the success of your enterprise. As such, it is very important for the CEO, or one of his senior managers, to influence and (to a degree) manage how these connections are established and maintained. Although a thorough treatment of this topic could consume an entire book, I want to focus on one dimension that is almost inescapable in modern, product innovation businesses – connection to the outside world through the Internet.

In 1945, Vannevar Bush, the first presidential science advisor who worked for both Franklin Roosevelt and Harry Truman, published a now-famous essay entitled "As We May Think" in which he, in essence, anticipated the coming of the Internet.[43] Fifty years later, by the mid-1990's, our daily lives had become revolutionized by ready access to information made available through the Internet, and our vocabulary had become forever changed with new verbs derived from Internet-based information-retrieval resources like Google and Mapquest.

Today, over sixty years since Vannevar Bush's prognostication, we are at the dawn of a second revolution of Web-based capability: the so-called Web 2.0 revolution. Whereas the first incarnation of the Internet - Web 1.0 - brought with it an enormous change in how we store, transfer, retrieve, and work with information, the second incarnation of the Internet - Web 2.0 - is rapidly changing how we interact with information, and indeed, how we interact with other people!

The new family of Web 2.0 capabilities that are becoming commonplace in our everyday life and that are revolutionizing our process of social interactions include: LinkedIn, Twitter, Facebook, etc. Indeed, Web 2.0 is mainly focused on *social computing* – a user-driven collaboration paradigm in which users assemble and organize themselves and work in partnership with a common goal in mind. In short, Web 1.0 was all about users interacting with information, and Web 2.0 is all about users interacting with other users.

Just as Web 1.0 revolutionized our private and corporate lifestyles (what companies could now exist without email?), Web 2.0 is poised to drive a second revolution in our private and corporate lifestyles. Within

---

[43] "As We May Think", Atlantic Monthly, July 1945, [http://www.theatlantic.com/doc/194507/bush]

the business sector, we are starting to see the concept of Web-based social networking become more commonplace, and Web 2.0 norms for the business sector are becoming codified through professional societies like "Enterprise 2.0".[44]

What effects could this second Internet revolution have on your enterprise? Most likely it will have dramatic effects. Indeed, a lesson that has been repeated often throughout this book is that mastering the various pieces to *The Inventor's Puzzle* requires you to avail yourself of outside resources. As stated before, the most successful entrepreneurs are very social people who built their successes through a very extensive network of colleagues, supporters, partners, and investors.

> If socializing and connecting with other people is a key to success in product innovation business, then the Web 2.0 revolution in the way we socialize and connect with other people is very likely to have a dramatic effect on future product innovation businesses.

I can think of numerous ways in which the Web 2.0 paradigm could help you streamline efforts to build your enterprise. Certainly, the very basic function of connecting with possible business partners, investors, and advisors, could be made dramatically more efficient through the use of networking programs like LinkedIn. Furthermore, the process of gathering early feedback from potential customer groups, which could be critical to defining a proper set of requirements for your product, could be made extremely efficient through the use of well-placed blogs, newsgroups, and/or other social-interaction protocols like Twitter.

Ultimately, the entire process of marketing and advertising will likely change from a *passive* approach (i.e., people read your ad), to an *interactive* approach (i.e., people read and react to your ad through a two-way protocol). If Web 1.0 made catalogued information *available at the speed of light*, Web 2.0 has the potential to make customer feedback and emotions *available at the speed of light!* Indeed, this capability could completely rewrite the book on how a product innovation business should market and sell its new products!

---

[44] http://www.e2conf.com/

I offer this perspective to you at this point in the book, because I believe this second Web-based revolution will become very critical to future product innovation companies. The shift in paradigm will be gradual, and certainly many companies will survive and thrive using the old norms and business practices. However, if you are forward thinking and comfortable in the use of some of these new Web 2.0 capabilities, I think you would be well served to have this capability become an explicit part of your enterprise plan. If you lack this expertise, you might consider bringing key people into your enterprise who are very conversant in the capabilities of Web 2.0, and who can help you create a strategy for best capitalizing on these capabilities within your enterprise.

Getting outside help

If, at this point, you are feeling a bit overwhelmed at the challenge of building up a company, don't worry – you are having a very healthy reaction to the reality of life as a product innovation CEO! Creating any business from the ground up is a difficult task, and creating one that is purpose-built to develop a particular invention into a marketable product is both difficult and risky! If you have no prior experience in starting or running a business, then you should be feeling uncomfortable and challenged by this particular piece of *The Inventor's Puzzle*. Every piece of the puzzle up until now required only a modest degree of risk, but this is the piece where failure becomes costly.

In all other chapters of this book, I have repeatedly extolled the virtues of not doing it alone. Furthermore, I started this chapter by citing John Donne's famous poem "No Man is an Island," and I did so because I knew that, if not before now certainly by now, you would be feeling uneasy about your own abilities to get your enterprise off of the ground. *You should feel uneasy, but you should not feel discouraged.* The uneasiness is a result of finally gaining a healthy and fairly complete perspective on the totality of the enterprise you are contemplating and the cost and risk of failing at the enterprise. It is the same uneasiness that every business leader feels at the outset of a new business enterprise. If dealt with appropriately, this uneasiness should be a source of motivation, not discouragement, and lead to sound decisions and decisive actions, rather than indecision and inaction.

In this section, I want to talk very explicitly about how you can take advantage of a variety of resources outside of your enterprise to help you launch and grow your enterprise. I will focus on three categories of outside help that you might consider: small-business incubators, societies of retired executives, and paid consultants. Although there are other organizations that can be helpful to your enterprise, these three types of organizations are some of the most-used in the world of product innovation startups, and they are somewhat complimentary and cover most of the wide-ranging needs you might have.

Small-business incubators. At the very beginning of your business enterprise, you can find that the "mechanics" of starting the business (e.g., renting space and setting up essential support functions) are time consuming, costly, and draining on your energy. Furthermore, this distraction can easily de-focus you from other critical early-stage business-development activities like networking and building relationships with future collaborators and investors. To help you manage and balance these early-stage needs, it might make sense to consider moving your business into a *business incubator* – an organization that is specifically designed to help businesses get started.

The primary goals of a business incubator are to produce successful businesses that are able to operate independently and are financially viable. Business incubators are specifically focused on very-early-stage startup businesses that need help and guidance getting off the ground. To accomplish this mission, business incubators usually provide:

Small-Business Incubator Resources

- Office and lab space at reasonable lease rates for up to two or three years.
- Common-use space like conference rooms, break rooms, and restrooms.
- Fee-based business support services like telephone and Internet, accounting, fax and copy machine access, etc.
- Group rates for health, life and other employee insurance plans.
- Business and technical assistance including: assistance in getting funding and networking with business advisory groups.

Business incubators have a wide variety of structures and supportive mechanisms. Roughly half of all incubators are nonprofit organizations, about a quarter are affiliated with a specific university, and the remaining quarter are either private (for profit) or some kind of hybrid effort between government and private organizations. The main reason that most business incubators exist is to provide an economic stimulus for the community by providing jobs and a means to expand the local business base.

Business incubators are rapidly becoming common starting points for product innovation companies throughout the country. Indeed, a growing number of incubators are privately funded and receive a piece of equity (often around 20% of the company) in the startup business in exchange for office space, $100,000 to $300,000 of startup capital, and ongoing business support. These types of incubators are extensions of private-investment groups and are usually staffed and supported by entrepreneurs who know a lot about getting a company off the ground and started in the right direction.

One down side of almost all business incubators is that the number of available slots is limited, and gaining entry into one can be a fairly involved process. It is not unusual for 10-20 applications to be reviewed for a single available slot in the incubator. As with any other kind of funding support, gaining entrance into a business incubator requires a compelling business case – a solid *elevator pitch!* Regardless of whether or not you are able to get into an incubator, just going through the process of applying and networking with the incubator director and staff could be a very valuable learning exercise.

Retired executive service organizations. Another growing trend in the small-business sector is for senior business executives, both actively employed and retired, to give back to the business community by volunteering a portion of their time to counsel with small businesses and business startups. Oftentimes these business experts have succeeded in several business enterprises of their own, made themselves fairly wealthy in the process, and are at a point in their career where they want to help younger entrepreneurs out for the simple pleasure of seeing others succeed in business as well.

Indeed, many business incubators, especially those that are structured as non-profit foundations, have established a network of retired and active business leaders within their local region, and draw upon that network of business experts to provide advice and guidance to companies within the incubator. Probably the largest national organization is the Service Corps of Retired Executives (SCORE)[45], which is a nonprofit association and a resource partner with the U.S. Small Business Administration (SBA). SCORE was founded in 1964 and is headquartered near Washington, DC with chapters throughout the United States.

An organization of retired executives can give you excellent free advice on basic issues that are critical to your startup business. Furthermore, these organizations will undoubtedly help you build your "rolodex" of professional contacts that might become critical to you as your business grows and evolves in the future.

Professional consultants. The final category of outside help that I want to address is that of paid professional business consultants. Of course, being a consultant myself, I would be remiss if didn't spend a little bit of time here discussing the pros and cons of this type of outside help! In general, these people are experienced in various aspects of the business-development problem, and they tend to be hired by a CEO to provide direct consultation services to the him. The range of services vary dramatically from consultant to consultant with some very focused on internal-operations issues (e.g., growing the team, human resource issues, etc.), and some very focused on business-strategic issues (e.g., intellectual property strategy, strategic partnering, etc.)

First I have to say that, just like the other two categories of outside support (business incubators and retired executive service groups), professional business consultants come in all "flavors," some good and some bad! Unfortunately, the bad ones tend to leave bad tastes in the mouths of their past clients, and this experience tends to create a lingering doubt and generally negative attitude towards the entire society of professional consultants! I say this just to let you know that, when you talk with other businesspeople about hiring the services of a paid consultant, you can expect to get strong opinions – sometimes strongly negative opinions!

---

[45] http://www.score.org/index.html

This said, I would like to add my own advice/guidance as to how to select between a good and bad consultant. First, I think the best way to find good consultants is through word-of-mouth. Quite possibly, the executives who you might meet through a business incubator or a senior executive service group will have had prior experiences with some good consultants, and can make specific recommendations to you. Second, you should always evaluate consultants just as rigorously you would a permanent employee. This means you should check references, have an interview or preferably multiple interviews, have a very specific set of goals or tasks that you want the consultant to perform and have them tell you how they will accomplish those tasks before you sign a contract.

Finally, you should always start any consulting agreement with a relatively modest initial contract (small in scope and time) during which you and the consultant can get to know each other better, and you can ultimately determine his or her value to your organization. If you approach the problem of finding a professional consultant in this way, you are most likely to be happy with the person you hire, and very likely to find the resource to be very beneficial to your growing enterprise.

> The main advantage to hiring a consultant over using free advisors you might find through an incubator or senior executive service group is that free advisors tend to only have a very limited amount of time to invest in your business, and they are most useful for their high-level advice and guidance. If you need someone who can help you on tactical issues (e.g., writing new business procedures, structuring your IP portfolio, training your employees on proper business practices, etc.) your needs will be best met by a consultant who is skilled in those areas, and who can spend an adequate amount of time addressing your needs in detail.

At the beginning of this section I said that if you have no prior experience in starting or running a business then you should be feeling uncomfortable and challenged by this particular piece of *The Inventor's Puzzle*. Many people like yourself have stood at a very similar juncture in their own enterprise and felt overwhelmed at the enormity and risk of launching their business. Luckily, you are not alone and have the benefit of numerous organizations around the country that can help hold your hand through the very early and formative stages of your business enterprise. Whether you find shelter in a local business incubator, guidance from a retired executive who is happy to meet with you once a month over coffee or dinner, or hands-on support from one or more professional consultants, availing yourself of these resources can be the difference between a startup that is launched in the right direction and a startup that ultimately fails to launch!

Summary

I started this chapter about the fifth and final piece of *The Inventor's Puzzle* by reciting John Donne's famous poem, "No Man is an Island." I chose this recitation because it evokes two different, and equally applicable, perspectives that are necessary to ensure one's success in the world of product innovation business.

First and true to the author's central theme in the poem, the world of product innovation business is, by definition, a community in which the success of one enterprise hinges on the success of other enterprises. For one to succeed does not necessarily require others to fail. Rather, one's success generally stems from a ground swell of success shared by several interconnected enterprises. Your enterprise is best positioned for success if it presents not only a good business opportunity for you, the inventor, but also for your team of employees, your investors, your strategic partners, and ultimately your customers! You cannot expect to succeed if any of them fail, and similarly you cannot fail if they all succeed!

Second and most obviously, John Donne's famous poem should provide you with another source of motivation as you stand at the beginning of your enterprise and look forward into what, inevitably, appears to be a complex and risky undertaking. You should not let your idea of building a business enterprise out of an invention stall out simply because you lack the personal knowledge and experience to move it forward. Take solace in the fact that you are not an "island" in your business enterprise as long as you avail yourself of the wide variety of resources that already exist in the business world and that are specifically designed to help startups *get started up* and to help later-stage companies *keep moving forward*!

If you now read "No Man is an Island" and feel more comfortable in knowing that you won't have to go it alone and you have mastered the issues and interconnections between the five pieces of *The Inventor's Puzzle*, then you have the wherewithal to create a successful business plan, and the maturity to get out, get known, and get moving on your enterprise. What then is left to learn in order to realize your vision of turning your invention into a marketable product? Well, just one last lesson – the lesson of how to succeed!

8

The Final Puzzle: Seeing the Deal and Dealing With the Unforeseeable

"Always bear in mind that your own resolution to succeed is more important than any other one thing."

–Abraham Lincoln

I started my career in the early 1980's as a research engineer for NASA – a job that brought me an enormous amount of pleasure and the opportunity to work with, and learn from the "best of the best" in this country's aerospace industry. However, by the late 1990's the Agency that I had loved since I was a kid had changed so dramatically for the worse that I decided to leave it for a second career in private industry.

A lot of things contributed to NASA's decline. But in my mind there was really one very critical element – a nearly complete stripping from the Agency's management structure of *vision and leadership*. During NASA's heyday of the 1960's it had grown tenfold in size and had accomplished the almost-unthinkable task of evolving the technology of spaceflight from the first 15 minute sub-orbital "hop" of Alan Shepard in 1961 to the spectacular first landing on the moon of Neil Armstrong and "Buzz" Aldrin in 1969. NASA was able to accomplish this for two reasons: 1) it was driven by a clear vision,[46] and 2) its management team consisted of people who refused to be defeated by failures.[47]

---

[46] On May 25, 1961, President John F. Kennedy announced before a special joint session of Congress the dramatic and ambitious goal of sending an American safely to the Moon before the end of the decade. [http://history.nasa.gov/moondec.html]

[47] *Failure is not an Option: Mission Control from Mercury to Apollo 13 and Beyond*, by Gene Kranz, Berkley Trade (2001)

When I started my career in the early 1980's, the remnants of this Apollo-era NASA were still there. But by the late 1990's, I had seen a blurring of vision combined with a changeover in the management chain from success-driven leaders to bureaucrats who were more driven by personal career ambition than the success of the organization. The net effect on that once-great Agency was to strip it of its capacity to perform miracles like it had in the 1960's. The net effect for me was to strip me of my desire to be part of that organization.

In the final days of my tenure with NASA and at the very time that I was becoming acutely aware of the critical role that leadership and vision plays in an organization, I happened to find a printed copy of a presentation by Colin Powell entitled "A Leadership Primer" thumb-tacked to a bulletin board at NASA's Jet Propulsion Laboratory. The presentation was one that Powell had given after his retirement as the Chairman of the Joint Chiefs of Staff under the first President Bush, and while he was on the public-lecture circuit prior to becoming the Secretary of State under the second President Bush.[48]

This presentation was a collection of eighteen lessons that the retired, four-star general had learned were key to effective leadership and management.[49] As I read through them, I could identify many specific examples within NASA where a lack of vision coupled with poor leadership abilities directly violated one, or several of Powell's eighteen leadership lessons. By the time I finished reading through the list, my decision to leave the Agency was final – I was convinced that I had no future in an organization that was stagnant due to lack of vision and leadership.

Why do I drag you through this particular episode of my personal life? Well, up until this point in the book, I have deciphered *The Inventor's Puzzle* into five pieces, and explored these pieces with enough detail that you are now much better equipped to develop a business plan and build a team that can execute the plan. At this point, I want to talk about two final aspects of product innovation business that are critical to your success and that will consume many hours of thoughtful contemplation and deliberation after you actually launch the enterprise. Addressing

---

[48] *My American Journey*, by Colin Powell with Joseph E. Persico, Random House (1995)
[49] For reference, I have included Gen. Powell's lessons on leadership at the end of this book.

these final aspects of the problem – constructing your end goal and finding the means to deal with unanticipated issues and challenges – constitutes a puzzle in and of itself and one that ultimately will define your success in product innovation business.

To start the discussion of this final puzzle, I can think of no better example than the one I lived through with NASA. Out of this highly capable institution populated by elite and talented individuals, I saw polar opposite results: programs that were successful in spite of unbelievable challenges, and those that were failures despite an unbelievable network of support. What caused such dramatically different outcomes? At the risk of over-simplifying a complex issue, I contend that the most significant factor separating success from failure was the presence, or absence, of vision and leadership.

> One thing that you can count on in the small business world is that *there is not one thing that you can count on!* Life in small business moves quickly and challenges come from multiple directions. You can plan for and address all of the issues presented in this book, but this alone is not sufficient to ensure your success. Those who succeed are also responsive, aware, creative, and capable of turning any bad circumstance – no matter how stark – into a path forward.

I once heard the leader of a startup medical-device company state that "the main requirements for being a CEO in a small company are: 1) a willingness to eat airport food, and 2) an ability to survive multiple, near-death experiences!" Indeed, success in small business is not just the end result of a carefully planned effort, success is the end result of a carefully constructed vision that has been adopted by an expertly led, well-managed, and very capable organization that refuses to fail.

In the last chapter I discussed how to build such a capable organization. In this chapter, I will discuss how to set that organization, and yourself, up for success by creating the right vision and establishing the right leadership principles to convert that vision into an *esprit de corps* among your team that will see the team through the inevitable difficult times ahead, and will instill in that team, and in you, the confidence to persevere even when times get tough.

You have to fail in order to succeed

There are many reasons why NASA should never have succeeded in landing twelve men on the moon in the late 1960's and early 1970's. Indeed, during that same time frame, a group of equally brilliant scientists and engineers in the former Soviet Union saw their own attempted moon missions fail miserably and their program collapse in despair while NASA took its own failures in stride and pressed onwards to prevail in what is arguably the greatest engineering achievement of the 20th century.

Why did NASA succeed while the Soviet space agency failed? Personally, I don't believe it was because of superior intellect, larger budgets, or some kind of political or ideological advantage. I think it was simply because everyone in the U.S. space program from the President down to the lowest technician absolutely demanded success, and believed that to be successful you had to experience and learn from failures.

Have you watched the movie "Apollo 13?" If not, then you can forget about all of the other movie references I have made if you will go out and buy a personal copy of that movie and watch it right now. There is one particularly pivotal moment in the movie when mission control manager Gene Krantz[47] (portrayed brilliantly by Ed Harris), frustrated by the steady stream of bad news, asks his colleagues to identify "what is working on the crippled spaceship?" It was at that critical moment, and driven by the solutions-oriented approach that defined Krantz's leadership style, that the process of rescue for the mission began and the path towards successful return of the crew was established. *It was at this moment, that NASA turned a tragic failure into an unbelievable success.*

> A hidden paradox in the business world is that the most successful businesses have failed miserably at one or more points in their history. Indeed, the secret to their ultimate success is in their ability to work through their own failures and press on with the advantage of very valuable lessons they learned.

In the 1960's NASA was dominated by a corps of leaders who, in the spirit of Gene Krantz, did not fear failure – they anticipated it, planned for it, and when it happened, they worked through it and learned from it. For Gene Krantz, failure of the mission, failure to succeed in the ultimate challenge of putting a man on the moon "was not an option." However, and as dramatically shown in the movie "Apollo 13," failure of a subsystem, a planned procedure, or an individual to succeed in his assigned task, was a daily occurrence. If failure was not an option for Gene Krantz, I guarantee that he would not have been the manager of NASA's mission control. Failure was his daily companion, and success over failure was his ultimate achievement!

In the military world, this mentality might be described as "losing a few battles in order to win the war." Indeed, it should not be surprising to know that Gene Krantz and much of the NASA management team, as well as all of the astronauts, in the 1960's were ex-military and very well disciplined in this principle! If you have military training, you should also accept this principle as instinctive. If you don't, then you can watch "Apollo 13" and read Colin Powell's Leadership Primer at the end of this book, and I think you will begin to appreciate the principle.

In my view, this is the simple reason why the United States beat the Soviet Union to the moon. More importantly, this will be the reason that your enterprise will ultimately be successful – that you and your team accept *a priori* that the best-laid plans will change and that, to be successful, you absolutely must become adept at expecting the unexpected and dealing with the inevitable challenges and "failures" along the way. If things will go wrong, if failure is almost a guaranteed daily companion in the world of product innovation businesses, then how do you deal with this and ultimately succeed?

Dealing with Predictable and Unpredictable Failures

1.   Understand how and when *predictable* failures are most likely to occur and develop *contingency plans* to put in place in the event of such a failure (i.e., always have a "plan B!")

2.   When unexpected things go wrong and you have no obvious plan forward, be ready to develop a new path forward in *real time* – right now, without hesitation.

The following two sections will discuss these two steps to deal with potential failures. First, I will talk about what can be done to anticipate predictable failures and how you can avoid such failures through proper planning. Second, I will talk about the unexpected crises that inevitably occur in all small-business enterprises, and what you can do to resolve these effectively as they occur.

Anticipation and planning – the keys to avoid *predictable* failures

George Santayana, the early 20th century Spanish philosopher once wrote: "Those who cannot remember the past are condemned to repeat it." This phrase and the numerous variations that we hear and repeat daily provide the main impetus behind my own love for the study of history. I am not drawn to the rote memorization of historical dates and facts, but rather the interpretive study of historical figures and events. I find in these people and their experiences a wealth of insights into the present and perspectives on the future. By this point in the book, you have doubtlessly figured out that I like history, and hopefully you have come to appreciate how looking backwards in time is a good way to see the path forwards.

Inspired by such an historical perspective, in this section I want to talk about *predictable* failure scenarios for small product innovation companies – the somewhat common ways in which such companies fail. More importantly, I want to discuss how such failures can be avoided through proper planning. In general, these predictable failures do not depend greatly on the particular product or market niche being served by the company. Rather, these failures tend to result from the basic evolutionary process that all companies undergo, and the essential dynamics of interacting with other companies within the business world. So the discussion here assumes no particular type of product or market, and should apply reasonably well to all products and markets.

First, I wish to talk about the potential predictable failure scenarios that result from inadequately addressing any of the five pieces of *The Inventor's Puzzle* described within this book. Indeed, as explained in Chapter 1, these five pieces of *The Inventor's Puzzle* were specifically constructed to address potential predictable failures that typically occur in product innovation businesses. By definition, addressing these issues thoroughly and adequately in your own enterprise is certain to help you avoid many of the usual scenarios in which such businesses tend to fail.

> Failure to adequately address the five pieces of *The Inventor's Puzzle* described within this book will likely lead to a failure of your enterprise – either immediately, or more likely down the road and after you and your investors have made a substantial investment in the enterprise.

For example, assume that you didn't do a good job of understanding what the customer wanted in your product (i.e., you failed to adequately address the issues described in Chapter 3), you will experience a predictable failure in your business after you have gone through all of the other steps (Chapters 4 through 7) and introduced a product in the market that simply isn't bought! This is a very late-stage failure that was rooted in an early-stage miscue.

Similarly, if you fail to secure a solid IP position around your product (Chapter 4), but succeed in all other issues presented in Chapter 3 and 5 through 7, you can expect to fail after you have introduced a very successful product and when the competition learns that they can steal your ideas and make money with them! This is an even later-stage failure that would have also been rooted in an early-stage miscue.

Alternatively, if you fail to lay out a proper product-development program (Chapter 6) or build the right team (Chapter 7), you can expect your enterprise to fail at some point within the product-development process, usually when you encounter a technical snag that was not anticipated and results in intolerable cost growth or outright failure of the design. Finally, if you fail to secure proper funding at any phase of your enterprise (Chapter 5), you can expect your enterprise to fail the instant that the last funding increment dries up!

In addition to the model offered within this book, I also would like to point you at two other well-known business models that have achieved a degree of success in helping entrepreneurs avoid predictable failures. The first alternative model is not specific to product innovation companies, whereas the second model is very specific to product innovation companies. I feel that both models, in addition to the five pieces of *The Inventor's Puzzle* offered here, provide a very comprehensive and complete view of the potential predictable failures that you might experience.

In 1990, Ichak Adizes introduced the concept of the *Corporate Lifecycle*,[50] as a model to describe how businesses grow, develop, and in some circumstances, fail. Although not written specifically for the product innovation business sector, the Adizes *Corporate Lifecycle* model overlays nicely on a product innovation startup, in that the company must evolve substantially from the moment of conception of the invention through all stages of product development, market introduction, and recurring sales and support.

In his book, Adizes explains how and why corporations grow and die through the stages of the corporate lifecycle. His analysis of each stage allows one to determine: 1) where the organization is now within its lifecycle, 2) what will be required to maintain the organization health within the current stage, and 3) what kinds of obstacles, perils, etc. can be expected as the organization moves into the next stage of its lifecycle.

One common failure scenario that Adizes describes occurs when the organization out grows the management team by moving into a stage of development beyond which the management team has the experience to effectively lead. In such a scenario the management team often reacts by nudging the organization backward in its evolution path and towards a state that is more familiar and comfortable with which to deal. Of course, such a move generally stifles the growing organization and halts its progress, which can lead to failure if left unchecked.

I will leave you to read Adizes book as a means to explore other specific failure scenarios that he describes; and here I will simply reiterate a few of the general points that he makes. First, Adizes identifies four critical

---

[50] *Corporate Lifecycles: How and Why Corporations Grow and Die and What to Do About It,* by Ichak Adizes, The Adizes Institute, (1990)

factors (performance, administration, entrepreneurship, and integration) that must be kept in balance while managing the company. Second, Adizes shows that the proper balance point for these factors will always be changing even within a single lifecycle stage because of internal and external forces that can bring about failure. Finally, Adizes states that, in order to avoid failure, the CEO or other business leaders must constantly be aware of what that ideal balance between these factors should be, and they must anticipate and plan for evolution of this balance point.

A third model that deals with corporate failure, and that is much more specific to the world of product innovation businesses was written by Geoffrey Moore and entitled *Crossing the Chasm*.[51] The essential thesis of Moore's book is that *mainstream* – high-volume – customers are generally cautious against buying new products that are very different than products they have purchased in the past. Indeed, any market can be divided into a few categories from the *early adopters* who will readily grab onto anything that is new and flashy, to the *late adopters* who will only buy a product many years after its first introduction, and after it has become the new market standard.

> The main conclusion of Moore's book is that most product innovation businesses fail because they only market to the small segment of *early adopters* and fail to fully understand the needs of the dominant and much larger remaining segments of the market.

Moore provides several specific examples of new products that failed simply because they never *crossed the chasm* of market acceptance from the *early adopter* mentality of "I will buy anything that is new and different" to the *late adopter* mentality of "I will only buy something new when it is the last resort." Although sales to the early adopter market could be significant and worthy of pursuit, in and of itself, Moore's main

---

[51] *Crossing the Chasm: Marketing and Selling Disruptive Products to Mainstream Customers,* by Geoffrey Moore, Collins Business Books (2006)

point is that ignoring the mainstream markets will lead to orders of magnitude lower sales and value growth in your intellectual property.

Certainly, the failure scenarios that are described in both Adizes' and Moore's books are later-stage scenarios – meaning that they are failures that your enterprise would not likely experience until it is well into the advanced stages of product development or marketing and sales. Nevertheless, these books both define root causes of these late-stage failures that start at much earlier stages of the startup enterprise. For example, Moore's book makes it very clear that your very early market-analysis work must address both the segment of people who will happily buy your product and the segment who will only buy it reluctantly. If you are to become most successful, you need to have something that even the reluctant will buy!

I heartily encourage you to read these additional books and talk more with other small-business experts about their experiences with failure scenarios. Don't let the discussion of business failure scenarios dissuade you from launching your own enterprise. Rather, let it help you improve your plans so you can eliminate or minimize the possibility of *predictable* failures in your enterprise. Then you can move forward with confidence and focus your daily attentions on those unexpected challenges that are almost certain to occur. Going back to a quote that I shared earlier in this chapter, a key qualification for the successful CEO is an ability to survive multiple, "near-death" experiences! Let's talk now about those sudden, "near-death" experiences that might not be easy to predict.

Judgment and action – the keys to deal with unpredictable challenges

First, I want to be clear that I am not going to, nor would it be possible for me to describe all of the possible daily challenges that you might encounter in your business. Challenges will come from many sources, and the most problematic sources of your challenges will be very specific to your product and market. In other words, the things that will be most confounding to a software-development company might be very different than those for a company making children's toys. So the essence of what I want to discuss in this section is how to deal with the unexpected challenges – whatever the cause, nature, and severity.

Earlier in this chapter I stated that to deal with the unexpected things that can and will go wrong in your business enterprise, and especially in moments when you have no obvious plan forward, *you must be ready to develop a new path forward in real time – right now, without hesitation*. This type of action is probably the most difficult action for most small-business owners to take. Indeed, in the moment of crisis it is most natural to drop back and take no action, as all paths forward might feel uncomfortable and likely to bring about a worsening of the situation rather than a relief. This reaction is understandable and very much like the reaction that many people feel in the moment of personal crisis – sit and wait and eventually the crisis will pass. Unfortunately, most things that bring on crisis in small business are *self-imposed* – the result of actions or the lack of actions on the part of the business leaders.

So in a moment when you feel that the business is in crisis, you absolutely must take action to change the situation that led to the crisis, or the crisis will naturally worsen – not naturally abate! However, in order to take action that makes sense and will change the situation for the better, you need to efficiently and quickly drop back, regroup, enlist the help and support of people who can provide helpful feedback (e.g., people who might be outside of the situation with fresh and unbiased perspectives), and ultimately assess the situation as Gene Krantz would - from a solutions-oriented perspective. In short, you must exercise good judgment and, although you might not see an option that you think is perfect, you must find an option that changes the status-quo and that will provide an alternative path forward.

Once you have made the commitment forward, closely monitor the situation and see if the changes are having the desired effect. If not, don't hesitate to alter course again and onto yet another possible solution path. Success requires you to have a certain ability to see forward and judge the options at hand, but most importantly, success depends on your ability to take action with firmness and conviction. Every step does not have to be the best step, and you might later regret some steps that you take. But to avoid taking action while you wish and hope for the situation to clear up is to fail and to lose the battle. Lose enough of the daily battles, and you are certain to lose the war. Lose just a few of the daily battles, and you are likely to win.

There are two very essential qualities that you, or the person you have chosen to lead your enterprise, must possess in order to deal effectively with the inevitable and unpredictable challenges. First, you must be able to assess the situation at hand and exercise a commonsense judgment over the possible consequences of alternative actions. Second, you must have a drive to take corrective action – you simply will not succeed by being passive and hoping that the storm will pass.

Commonsense Judgment. In the Preface to this book, I established a goal to replace some ignorance with knowledge that can allow you to create a new *common sense* about the business world - a perspective from which you can more instinctively anticipate issues and problems as they are about to occur, and more efficiently act to put these issues to rest. I chose the phrase *common sense* very intentionally, but for reasons that might not yet be obvious. So at this point, think it is important to talk directly about what I mean by *common sense*.

In one definition the phrase *common sense* refers to "beliefs or propositions that most people would consider prudent and of sound judgment, without reliance on esoteric knowledge or study or research, but based upon what they see as knowledge held by people 'in common'."[52] Consistent with this definition, I consider the collection of beliefs and propositions presented in this book to be *common sense*, as they reflect what is considered to be prudent and of sound judgment within the small, product innovation business world.

Indeed, this book has not been an attempt to write new theories for the small, product innovation business sector. It is an attempt to distill the general policies and practices of that sector into a concise set of issues (five to be exact), that best capture the essential ingredients of success, and to present those issues in a manor that makes it easy for the reader to see how they are *common sense*.

If any of the beliefs or propositions presented here seem strange or unusual to you at first, it is simply a reflection of your relative lack of experience in this business sector. I suspect that readers of this book

---

[52] http://en.wikipedia.org/wiki/Common_sense

who have had significant experiences in this business sector will read these chapters with a smile on their face, and a slight wink and a nod to themselves in recognition of how truthful the examples are, and how critical the issues are to success.

> *"The three great essentials to achieve anything worthwhile are, first, hard work; second, stick-to-itiveness; <u>third, common sense</u>.*"
>
> – Thomas Edison

I love this quote from Thomas Edison, the man who I have already acknowledged to be, arguably, the most prolific and successful inventor that our country has ever produced. I love this quote more than quote I cited at the beginning of Chapter 1, because this quote acknowledges a key element that is missing from that, more famous quote – the element of *common sense or judgment*. Inspiration and perspiration aside, your business enterprise is doomed for failure if your decisions, the very decisions that will launch efforts resulting in endless hours of perspiration, are not rooted in a sound judgment and mature perspective on what works and what doesn't work in the small, product innovation business sector.

Since you are still with me, eight chapters later, it is clear that you are someone who has a desire to become more experienced in the small-business world. Maybe you have already taken some steps towards marketing your ideas, or begun to think about how you could actually create a product from your ideas.

Do you already have the necessary business common sense and good judgment to see the best paths forward in times of crisis? If you have already had discussions with business people about your ideas, and you have gotten a lukewarm feeling back from these people, it is very likely that they have seen big holes in your plan – holes that, prior to reading this book, you might not have been so well-educated as to see yourself. Possibly, you have already talked with potential investors, who failed to see a well-defined intellectual-property position or a clear statement of the market need. Possibly, you have talked with a potential strategic partner, who failed to see a clear set of product-development requirements, and a convincing plan for getting the product to market. It is possible that any of these potential business partners who might have given you little consideration, are simply looking at the fact that you have no significant experience yourself, and few ideas about how to create the proper team to move forward.

> All successful businesses are built on well-accepted practices and principles, which collectively become instinctive or common sense to those in business. So if you have already had criticisms of your potentially immature business ideas, understand that this is likely a reflection of a relative lacking of commonsense judgment for business. Ultimately, whether this commonsense judgment comes from you or from your CEO or from key advisors to your business, it is critical that the judgment exists within and drives the leadership team. If you have it – great! If you don't – recognize this deficiency and surround yourself with, and rely on, people who have these commonsense principles well-ingrained in their minds, and for whom the process of assessing paths forward is an almost instinctive result of this common sense.

Action. Let me start this discussion with another short history lesson that will get right to the central point of the topic. In the early days of the Civil War, and after several early failures on the battlefield, Abraham Lincoln decided to promote a relatively young, energetic, and very popular general – George McClellan – to the post of supreme commander of the Union armies.[53] As a graduate of West Point, McClellan was well schooled in the principles of warfare. Moreover, McClellan was charismatic and extremely popular among both his troops and the politicians who oversaw various aspects of the military campaign. So it was appropriate and reasonable that Lincoln chose to entrust the security of the Union to Gen. McClellan's command.

Unfortunately, McClellan suffered from a lack of ability to see and effectively react to the rapidly changing situation in the Confederate States. Rather than taking action in response to the crisis of the day, McClellan suffered from what some historians refer to as *analysis paralysis* – a total consumption with analyzing the "what ifs" and an inability to select and execute an effective course of action. Prior to and

---

[53] *The Army of the Potomac: Mr. Lincoln's Army*, by Bruce Catton, Doubleday and Company, Inc. (1962)

during the early months of his command, this fatal flaw in his character was not apparent, as his responsibilities were mainly focused on training his troops for eventual battle. However, once met with the chaos and unpredictability that is inherent in warfare, it became utterly clear that McClellan was unfit to command.

Standing as almost the polar opposite of McClellan, Ulysses S. Grant was generally unpopular due to his lack of formal education, his poorly kept appearance, and his caustic interpersonal style. But for all of his deficiencies, Grant possessed the singular quality that Lincoln most needed – Grant was absolutely intolerant of inaction and indecision. Grant did not win every battle, and he made many now-famous blunders along the way. But Grant ultimately won the war and restored the Union, achieving the vision that Lincoln had established so clearly at the outset of the war, but that had evaded McClellan and a succession of similarly incompetent commanders who came before him.

> Whether you prefer to think of the rough and rumpled image of Ulysses S. Grant, or the white-starched and clean-cut image of Gene Krantz, you must appreciate that to take action means to be decisive and firm in a conviction that standing still will lead to certain failure. How long can you afford to debate the possible actions and judge the possible consequences of those actions? In some cases, (e.g., Grant's effort to win the war), you might have weeks or even months to assess the situation and respond with a new action. In other situations, (e.g., Krantz' effort to bring the Apollo 13 astronauts home safely) you might only have minutes or hours to act. The time constant for assessment is part of the judgment that is necessary and that should be instinctive to the seasoned small-business leader.

Seeing the end goal – creating your exit strategy

Implicitly throughout this book I have assumed that you, the inventor or would-be entrepreneur, have a clear vision for what you want to accomplish through the development and marketing of your invention. In general, I have assumed, and it would be reasonable to assume, that you wish to make money from your invention and that to do so requires that you must either build up some type of business enterprise around your invention or secure a solid IP portfolio around your invention and sell the rights to another company. Beyond that, I have tried to make no other assumptions about your vision and end goal for the enterprise. At this point as we near the end point of the book, it is absolutely essential that I now talk about this end goal. For without a clear vision of the end goal, it is impossible to ever achieve that end goal!

What are the possible exit strategies? Certainly, through the course of this book I have discussed several very specific end goals for your enterprise. For example, I have talked about assembling a product-development team to refine your design and prepare it for marketing and sales. Furthermore, I have discussed a variety of methods by which you could ultimately sell a product that your business might develop, including through your own, in-house staff of marketing and sales agents or through a strategic partnership with a larger company who already has an established distribution and sales network. Finally, in Chapter 4 I talked about how your IP portfolio could be sold or licensed outright to an existing company who wanted to develop and market a product from the beginning.

All of these scenarios are common within the product innovation business world, but deciding which one best-meets your needs is critical if you are to actually succeed. Just as it is important to be decisive in reaction to the short-term and daily challenges of business life, you must be clear in establishing your end goal. To say that "you want to be successful" by itself is nothing more than saying that you have a dream. To say that you want to build a very specific type of enterprise around your invention, and become successful in capitalizing on your invention through that enterprise is the beginning of a business plan.

> The place to start in building your business enterprise is to identify the place where you wish it to end.

By "end" I don't mean the point where your business fails, but rather the point when you cash out and leave the business to follow your next pursuit in life. To see this end goal requires that you first see all of the possible types of businesses that you might build around your invention and decide which of the possible business-development paths is most attractive to you. In the world of business, the end goal that you decide upon is called your *exit strategy*. "Exit" because it defines the point where you will ultimately exit from the enterprise that you have created. "Strategy" because to actually achieve this end goal requires a great deal of thoughtful planning and purposeful execution.

What is your exit strategy? Maybe you have had a clear idea of this from the outset. Maybe you have no interest in owning a business and are only interested in selling or licensing your intellectual property to the highest bidder. If not I might ask: did you get into this in order to become an expert in business, or did you get into this in order to get your invention into a market? The goal for most people is the latter, but many people become entangled in the details and daily challenges, and ultimately find themselves on a path for the former without ever recognizing that they chose that path, or more likely, failed to choose an alternate path!

> The more clearly you can define your exit strategy, the more easily you will be able to construct a plan to achieve it. If you are the type of person who likes to keep all options open, just beware that by doing so with your exit strategy you will likely de-focus your efforts and prevent yourself from ever exiting the enterprise.

Several times throughout this book I have talked about the importance of your elevator pitch – your concise summary of the business opportunity that your invention represents. You will find that your exit strategy will become just as essential to your elevator pitch as all other elements of the business plan.[54] Indeed, by now you appreciate that any type of enterprise that you build around your business will, by definition, involve people other than yourself, and you must accept that they will be driven by the same goal that drives you – to make money with the invention. As such, it is critical that they understand your

---

[54] *The McGraw-Hill Guide to Writing a High-Impact Business Plan: A Proven Blueprint for First-Time Entrepreneurs*, by James Arkebauer, McGraw-Hill (1994), pp. 120-122.

personal exit strategy and how it affects their ability to be successful in the enterprise.

Ultimately, most successful business leaders make a very conscious decision of when and how to leave. Once this goal is set, their efforts to achieve that goal are very focused and determined and transparent to all of their partners in the enterprise. If you are the inventor and creator of the idea around which the business will be built, your paternal tie to the invention is both your biggest strength and your biggest weakness. From it you derive endless hours of energy and enthusiasm to move on. Because of it you probably find it hard to imagine ever letting go.

Start your journey forward by imagining the day that you will let go of your invention and/or the business that you will build to market that invention. Visualize the person or organization to whom it will be transferred and become transparent with your motives and vision. If you can do this, then you will have saved others in your enterprise the frustration of puzzling over your vision. Indeed, you will attract others who see and want to become part of your vision, and in doing so you will go a long way towards creating the team who will help you realize that vision!

Summary

Every day, it is important for you to ask yourself "what have I done today that has moved the effort forward." If you don't already have it, develop a hatred for stagnation and intolerance for inaction. In small business, you absolutely MUST keep moving forward. Although the direction forward might change with changing events, the definition of forward does not. *Forward* is any direction that moves you closer to your end goal of commercializing your product or ideas.

At the beginning of this book I acknowledged that the single most powerful force in an inventor's journey forward is the passion he has for his own ideas and inventions. He has given birth to these ideas, and has the most deeply rooted motivation to see them become commercial products. Whether you are the inventor or the entrepreneur who will help build the business around the invention, never lose sight of that passion, as it will serve as your compensation on the days when nobody else is paying the bills. However, never allow the passion for the invention alone to overwhelm and drive your business decisions.

Passion without vision and action is nothing more than a dream, and the world of product innovation business is a world full of lost dreams. If you are serious about following your dreams, then become serious about learning what it takes to realize those dreams, and become committed to taking those steps.

The Final Puzzle: Seeing the Deal and Dealing With the Unforeseeable

Epilogue

Most people who become involved in product innovation business are attracted to the excitement of the unknown unknowns that are inherent to such enterprises. Whether that excitement stems from discovering a new idea for a product or identifying a new market opportunity for that product, most product innovation businesspeople are in it for the joy that comes from doing it for the first time. This book has not been an attempt to decipher the world of product innovation business to the point that there are no unknown unknowns. Indeed, no book could ever accomplish such a goal.

If there is an essential lesson of this book it is to recognize that, if you are new to the world of product innovation business, there are many things that might be unknown to you but that are quite common to others more experienced in this business sector. While you will find many challenges that will require a new invention or the invention of a new market niche, you must also realize that many questions that are causing you to stay up all night and that are preventing you from moving your ideas and inventions forward might be easily answered by looking outside of your own current experience base. If you are staying up all night looking for the answers to such questions it's likely that you could exhaust yourself (and possibly your bank account) in getting the answers through the school of hard knocks.

In engineering school, I was taught that in order to solve a difficult problem you must first be able to break it down into several smaller, less-difficult problems and then attack each of those problems separately. In my career I have encountered numerous people who, despite a great deal of intelligence, suffer from a lack of ability to effectively break down hard problems into solvable problems. Instead of seeing through complexity and simplifying the situation into something more manageable, they tend to focus on complexity and allow it to bring their forward progress to a halt. On the other hand, I have encountered many people who, without substantial formal education, have built amazingly successful businesses and professional careers through an Edison-like combination of hard work, stick-to-itiveness, common sense, and a keen ability to solve hard problems.

Through these associations, I have come to understand a little more about the intrinsic qualities that drive people to be successful in product innovation business. As you begin your journey into this exciting business sector you should gravitate towards people who are successful, and begin to absorb directly from them the additional insights that will help you become more successful. As a means to help you start building your professional "rolodex" of mentors, I have offered up a somewhat obscure historical figure, Filippo Brunelleschi, who epitomizes personal drive and success in product innovation business. I hope that his example, as well as the several better-known individuals that I have brought into the discussion throughout the book, will help you see more clearly what will be necessary for you to achieve success in your endeavors.

Endnote:
"A Leadership Primer" from Colin Powell[55]

Lesson 1:   "Being responsible sometimes means pissing people off."

Lesson 2:   "The day soldiers stop bringing you their problems is the day you have stopped leading them. They have either lost confidence that you can help them or concluded that you do not care. Either case is a failure of leadership."

Lesson 3:   "Don't be buffaloed by experts and elites. Experts often possess more data than judgment. Elites can become so inbred that they produce hemophiliacs who bleed to death as soon as they are nicked by the real world."

Lesson 4:   "Don't be afraid to challenge the pros, even in their own backyard."

Lesson 5:   "Never neglect details. When everyone's mind is dulled or distracted the leader must be doubly vigilant."

Lesson 6:   "You don't know what you can get away with until you try."

Lesson 7:   "Keep looking below surface appearances. Don't shrink from doing so (just) because you might not like what you find."

Lesson 8:   "Organization doesn't really accomplish anything. Plans don't accomplish anything, either. Theories of management don't much matter. Endeavors succeed or fail because of the people involved. Only by attracting the best people will you accomplish great deeds."

---

[55] http://www.chally.com/enews/powell.html

Lesson 9:	"Organization charts and fancy titles count for next to nothing."
Lesson 10:	"Never let your ego get so close to your position that when your position goes, your ego goes with it."
Lesson 11:	"Fit no stereotypes. Don't chase the latest management fads. The situation dictates which approach best accomplishes the team's mission."
Lesson 12:	"Perpetual optimism is a force multiplier."
Lesson 13:	"Powell's Rules for Picking People: Look for intelligence and judgment, and most critically, a capacity to anticipate, to see around corners. Also look for loyalty, integrity, a high energy drive, a balanced ego, and the drive to get things done."
Lesson 14:	"Great leaders are almost always great simplifiers, who can cut through argument, debate and doubt, to offer a solution everybody can understand."
Lesson 15:	"Part I: 'Use the formula P=40 to 70, in which P stands for the probability of success and the numbers indicate the percentage of information acquired.' Part II: 'Once the information is in the 40 to 70 range, go with your gut.'"
Lesson 16:	"The commander in the field is always right and the rear echelon is wrong, unless proved otherwise."
Lesson 17:	"Have fun in your command. Don't always run at a breakneck pace. Take leave when you've earned it: Spend time with your families. Corollary: surround yourself with people who take their work seriously, but not themselves, those who work hard and play hard."
Lesson 18:	"Command is lonely."

Index of Key Terms